# SEXUAL ABUSE:
## Causes, Consequences and Treatment Of Incestuous and Pedophilic Acts

Adele Mayer

**LP** Learning Publications, Inc.
Holmes Beach, Florida

Library of Congress Cataloging in Publication Data

Mayer, Adele.
    Sexual abuse.

    Bibliography: p.
    Includes index.
    1. Child molesting.  2. Incest.  3. Pedophilia.
3. Sexually abused children.  I. Title.  [DNLM: 1. Child
Abuse.  2. Incest.  3. Paraphilia.  4. Sex Offenses.
WA 320 M468s]
RC560.C46M38   1985          616.85'83          85-4610
ISBN 0-918452-80-5

**Learning Publications, Inc.**
**PO Box 1326**
**Holmes Beach, FL 33509**

Cover Design by Barbara J. Wirtz

Printing:   2 3 4 5 6 7 8   Year:     7 8 9

Printed and bound in the United States of America.

# Acknowledgment

The author wishes to thank Edsel Erickson, Lois Carl, and Danna Downing for their support, encouragement, and invaluable assistance in the development and production of this book.

# Table of Contents

# Preface

Until recently, therapists and other interested professionals have had difficulty finding resources for working with victims of child sexual abuse. Valid and reliable research studies, guidelines for treatment and case management, and information on prevention in the area of child sexual abuse simply did not exist. To those authorities who acknowledged the existence of the problem, whether perceived as real or fantasized by victims, child sexual abuse was linked to a few theories that now largely are held in disrepute. Studies were based on anecdotal rather than substantive data; population samples were small; and methodological errors in data analysis abounded. Generalizations were made from limited data derived from samples drawn from small segments of the population in terms of age, socioeconomic class, ethnic background and locale. Among the more popular theories of the day were those based on Freud's seduction theory and on the notion of victim precipitation.

Fortunately, the situation has changed drastically in recent years as we are developing an awareness of the immensity of the problem of child sexual abuse—an awareness that focuses not just on victims but also on family dynamics and deviant adult behavior. We now have a number of valid and reliable statistical studies relating to child molestation. From these studies we are able to provide documentation to assist victims and their families. We now know that there is a child sexual abuse syndrome resulting from molestation. We now know that recanting among victims is a common occurrence stemming from fear of retaliation by family members or fear of the court process. We also know that most children do not lie when disclosing molestation; that young child victims present themselves as credible witnesses in court; and that there are definite personality factors leading to favorable or poor prognoses for sex offenders.

Even though we now have a substantial body of literature dealing with child sexual abuse, we continue to need more information, particularly on treatment and prevention. We need to refine and redevelop the materials we do have in order to better meet the needs of child victims. The statistics are becoming more and more frightening as we see alarming increases in reported cases of incestuous abuse, extrafamilial molestation and child rape. Increasing numbers of psychologists, therapists, counselors and social workers are identifying and attempting to deal with the problem which is perceived to be a national epidemic of the 1980's—an epidemic whose scope and magnitude are still of unknown proportions.

SEXUAL ABUSE offers educational and human service professionals a broad overview of the causes, effects and treatment implications of child sexual abuse, as well as the types and patterns of behavior of sexual offenders. Case management, a vital and often neglected area of consideration in treatment manuals, is emphasized since child sexual abuse is more than a therapeutic issue.

Because incestuous abuse and extrafamilial molestation often involve physical as well as psychological trauma, and because these offenses are crimes, a coordinated team approach is explored at length. It is imperative that such an approach be used for the greatest benefit to the victims of these horrendous acts. The coordinated approach involves the participation and cooperation of knowledgeable health, educational, legal and social service personnel, all of whom function as a team to meet the specific goals of assisting young victims and reducing their trauma.

An important portion of this book is devoted to prevention. Many multi-media prevention materials have been developed for use with young children. Many of those used most effectively with youngsters are listed in the appendix. Professionals and parents alike should become familiar with the resources available. We all have a part to play. In the absence of stronger legislation, prevention is our only means to reducing the extent of child sexual abuse at the present time. Finally, resources and referrals are included in this text as an aid to professionals interested in expanding and deepening their knowledge and expertise in the field.

# 1

# Overview and Profile of Offenders

**Billy**: *I don't want to talk about Joe. He was dumb.*

**Counselor**: *You're angry at him.*

**Billy**: *No, I'm not. Sometimes he was nice. He was stupid. Dumb. A jerk.*

**Counselor**: *Did he ever threaten you?*

**Billy**: *He told me he'd leave me in the desert if I told anyone.*

**Counselor**: *Sounds as if you were too scared to tell. Did you want to tell anyone?*

**Billy**: *Sometimes he was nice. He gave me things. He was nice to me.*

**Counselor**: *Maybe you had mixed feelings about Joe—liked him and disliked him at the same time. What would you say to him if he were here now?*

**Billy**: *I'd kill him.*

Ambivalence, anger, guilt and shame are evident in this short, verbatim dialogue between a counselor and an eight-year-old victim of sexual molestation. Billy's nineteen-year-old male babysitter had sexually abused him for two years. The boy indicates to his counselor that he wants to talk about what happened and yet he does not. His words express anger but he denies experiencing negative feelings. Billy avoids the question of disclosure, possibly due to guilt because he had been silent about the molestation for two years. Intensive, patient, long-term therapy is needed to help this youngster begin to unravel his confused emotions.

Billy was one of the lucky victims of sexual molestation— lucky because disclosure did occur, because the family was supportive and believed the boy, and because the offender was arrested, thus validating, for Billy, the unlawfulness of the molestation.

The sexual abuse of children takes many forms, from incest within the home to rape by a stranger. Daily, children are being sexually abused and exploited in staggering numbers in this country. Therefore, it is imperative that mental health professionals, physicians, nurses and teachers become knowledgeable about the causes, signs, symptoms and intervention procedures that can minimize the traumatic effects of this national epidemic. In order to do this it is important that there be a clear understanding of the similarities and differences involved with each type of sexual abuse.

## Types of Sexual Abuse

Distinctions among the varieties of child sexual abuse can be artificial and misleading due to an overlapping among offenses.*

---

* Gene Abel, psychiatrist at the Sexual Behavior Clinic of the New York State Psychiatric Institute reports that forty-four percent of incest offenders admit to molesting other children and eighteen percent admit to forcible rape. (Reported in: Stark, E. "The Unspeakable Family Secret," *Psychology Today*, May, 1984.)

Nonetheless, to enhance our understanding of the problem, authorities distinguish between two broad categories—*incest*, and *extrafamilial molestation*. Incest or intrafamilial molestation, is sexual abuse that occurs within the family among family members. There are various manifestations of incestuous abuse from touching of a sexual nature, fondling, digital or vaginal penetration to rape. Also included in the definition of incest are the verbal stimulation and photographing of nude children within one's family.

Incest may occur only once or last for a period of months or years. A man who french kisses his twelve-year-old daughter only one time is guilty of incestuous abuse just as a father who has sexual intercourse with his teenage daughter for five years is guilty. The main variables in the two cases relate to the degree of abuse, the frequency and the intent.

Extrafamilial molestation of children is sexual molestation occurring outside of the family where the offenses usually are perpetrated by child lovers. The general term for a child lover is pedophile and the activity in which the offender engages is called pedophilia.

There are four general categories of sexual molestation of children outside of the family. The first category is physical molestation which may occur only one time or last for a period of years. Physical molestation covers a wide range of activities and can take the forms of fondling, oral copulation or anal and vaginal intercourse. The second category of extrafamilial molestation involves soliciting or exploiting children for the purposes of prostitution. Child prostitution involves the sale of children for immoral purposes. The third category of extrafamilial molestation involves engaging or helping to engage the child or children in pornographic activities. Child pornography is the use of children under the age of fourteen in photographs, tapes or films depicting lewd, lascivious and sexual activities. All three of these activities (molestation, prostitution, and pornography) can occur concomitantly and often do. A pedophile can be engaging in sexual acts with a child whom he photographs for private and/or commercial purposes and for whom he also pimps.

A final category of child sexual abuse (intra- or extrafamilial) is child rape. Frequently child rape is a crime perpetrated by someone who is known to the family. When the assailant is known to the victim, he is sometimes a relative and the offense is incestuous. If the offender is someone known, the assaults usually occur in the victim's or offender's homes during the daylight hours and they involve a wide range of sexual offenses including genital, anal and oral sex.

A number of child rapes are perpetrated by strangers. The child may be on the way home from school, the park, or the store when the perpetrator approaches him or her. Child rape rarely receives publicity because of the implications for both the child and the offender. Children are poor witnesses in court and offenders are rarely convicted or sentenced. According to Geiser, one out of every five rape victims in this country is under the age of twelve. A child rape occurs once every 45 minutes in the United States. The mean age for child rape victims appears to be ten or eleven; but victims have been as young as a few hours old.*

Victims of child rape usually are bribed, manipulated and sometimes threatened. If the offender is a stranger, he may physically harm the child. Incestuous offenders usually do not hurt their victims deliberately; nevertheless, young children who are raped do suffer from a variety of physical consequences including lacerations, bruises, and vaginal or anal enlargement. As with other forms of child sexual abuse, child rape is not linked to socio-economic class, race or ethnic status.

When we consider the prevalence of these crimes against children and the various types of abuse (incest, molestation outside of the home, prostitution, pornography and brutal rape), we begin to see the extent of this problem. Because of the magnitude of child

* Geiser, R. L. *Hidden Victims: The Sexual Abuse of Children.* Boston: Beacon Press, 1979, p. 20.

sexual abuse, it is essential to enlighten and educate professionals and their communities so that they can intervene on behalf of the helpless victims.

## Extent of the Problem

Statistics regarding the prevalence of incestuous abuse in the United States are unreliable. At this time the data is not sufficient to indicate for sure whether or not incest is increasing, although many professionals suspect that it is. However, it is a fact that there has been an alarming rise in the number of cases reported.* This increase is suspected as being partly due to social changes such as declining morals and an increase in the portrayal of all forms of sexual expression in the mass media. Furthermore, authorities believe that there is an increase not only in incestuous abuse but in the manifestations of this abuse. Incest combined with physical abuse, torture and/or a variety of "kinky" activities appears to be on the rise. Therapists report seeing children who have been brutally raped by relatives while tied to bedposts or following physical beatings. In one recent case, a father tied his young sons to posts and threw knives at them following episodes of sodomy.

Nonetheless, we do not have reliable data on any of the several forms of incestuous abuse. There are many reasons for this. In the first place, in many states, child sexual abuse is reported under the broad category of child abuse. Secondly, many families and authorities are reluctant to report incest because it is against the law and remains the "last taboo." Horror and shock are evoked when people hear of incest.

---

* David Finkelhor of the Family Violence Research Program at the University of New Hampshire, reports that two to five million American women have had incestuous relations. Nineteen percent of all American women and nine percent of the men were sexually abused as children. (Reported in: "A Hidden Epidemic," *Newsweek*, May 14, 1984.)

People become defensive about incest and begin to react with denial because the very topic appears to trigger identification and a need to defend and protect adult peers. One therapist reported to authorities a case of incest involving breast fondling and exhibitionism, and the response was, "Is that all he did?" One wonders if the same form of denial that permeates the incestuous family also permeates the larger society as a whole.

Leading authorities in the field of child sexual abuse believe that at least one in ten families is involved in incestuous abuse, and this figure may be a conservative one.* There is a strong likelihood that incest is occurring in every neighborhood throughout the nation. According to Geiser, for every incest case reported, another 25 remain hidden.

Lucy Berlinger of the Harborview Hospital, Seattle, is an authority on child sexual abuse. Her data indicates that one in four females will be sexually assaulted before she reaches the age of eighteen.** (Here, sexual assault includes rape, incest, and extrafamilial molestation of children). Geiser reports that one in eight boys is sexually abused before the age of eighteen. Finkelhor's data suggest one in eleven male juveniles will be molested.*** The vast majority of victims of incestuous abuse are females and approximately 98% of the perpetrators are males (usually fathers, stepfathers, grandfathers, brothers, uncles and live-in boyfriends who assume a parent role). In addition, the extent of the problem of incest is reflected in the high correlations between child molestation and prostitution, and child molestation and chemical abuse. In Densen-Gerber's study of 118 female chemical abusers, 44% were victims of incest and 75% reported having been sexually

---

* Geiser, R. L. *Hidden Victims: The Sexual Abuse of Children*. Boston: Beacon Press, 1979, p. 46.

** Numerous authorities concur with this estimate, among them: Weber, E. "Sexual Abuse Begins At Home," *Ms. Magazine*, April, 1977, p. 64.

*** Finkelhor, D. *Sexually Victimized Children*. New York: The Free Press, 1979.

abused before the age of nine.* Elias reported that 75% of his sample of 200 street prostitutes had been raped as children.** As reported in the *Journal of Humanistic Psychology* (Fall, 1978, #18), of 160 women treated for sexual dysfunction, 90% had been raped during childhood, and 23% were raped by fathers or stepfathers.*** Sexual abuse is one of the three main reasons children run away from home.

As with incestuous abuse, statistics regarding extrafamilial molestation are difficult to compile and consequently underestimate the problem. Authorities believe that most cases of extrafamilial molestation are not reported partly because victims are reluctant to disclose the fact that they have been molested. In almost all cases the victim feels guilty and ashamed. On the other hand, the child victim may be afraid to report abuse because of the fear of rejection by a pedophile who offers love. The child often feels a deep loyalty toward the perpetrator. There have been cases where the police have detained a child prior to arresting the pedophile for fear that the young victim would warn the offender that there was a warrant out for his arrest.

If a child does disclose sexual abuse to his or her parent, the parent often fails to report it to the authorities. Current researchers believe that up to 75% of those parents who have reason to believe that their child was molested do not report it. Sometimes the parents do not believe their child; or they may be afraid of the publicity or trauma associated with a possible court hearing.

There are records which indicate that there are at least two million pedophiles in the United States. However, Lloyd Martin, a prominent expert in the field of sexual molestation of children, believes that the figures are much higher and that 90% of the cases

---

* Densen-Gerber, J. "The Big Issue." New York: Odyssey House, July 1, 1977.

** Elias, T. "Young Female Prostitutes," *The Press*, Vol. 10, # 5, October, 1982.

*** Giarretto, H. "The Humanistic Treatment of Father-Daughter Incest." *Journal of Humanistic Psychology*, Fall, 1978, p. 18.

of extrafamilial molestation remain unreported.* Each pedophile can victimize an average of 50 children in his lifetime. Some children are molested only once; others are involved in pedophilic relationships for months or even years; and some children, molested early in childhood, are re-molested by different pedophiles later in childhood.

For every victim of incest, there are an estimated ten victims of extrafamilial molestation. Clearly, the problem is staggering. Martin's research indicates that 32 to 46 percent of all children are sexually assaulted by the age of eighteen. While the majority of the victims of incestuous abuse are female, most of the victims of pedophilia are pre-adolescent males, although a large number of females are also molested. The perpetrators in most cases are male although there are some female pedophiles.

The problem of extrafamilial molestation is compounded by the fact that pedophiles are rarely detected or apprehended. Roxxman reports that in a study of one thousand pedophiles, less than one percent had been arrested. Of those arrested, less than three percent were incarcerated.**

Childhood prostitution is rampant in the United States. About 50% of the estimated 600,000 juveniles involved in prostitution nationwide are male. Betz reports that between 1969 and 1978 the number of boys working the streets rose 245% as compared to a 183% increase for girls.***

Seven percent of the pornography market in the United States consists of child pornography. Child pornography constitutes a multi-million dollar business. A child often becomes involved in pornography following sexual abuse by a pedophile. One youngster was enticed into the home of a man in the neighborhood, ostensibly

---

* Martin, L. and Haddad, J. *We Have A Secret*. Newport Beach, CA: Crown Summit Books, 1982, p. 7.

** Roxxman, P. *Sexual Experience Between Men and Boys*. New York: Association Press, 1976.

*** Betz, B. "Young Male Hustlers." *The Press*, Vol. 10, #5, October 1982, p. 28.

to see his toy train collection. Within a few months, an assortment of local children were visiting the home, all engaging in sexual activities together and being photographed for private and commercial use.

There is a vast international network supporting pedophilia. A number of groups actively promote the legalization of sex with minor children. One group, the Rene Guyon Society, with a membership of about 8,500, boasts as its credo, "Sex before eight or else it's too late."* Members advocate child-child and child-adult sexual activity. They claim that western civilization has inculcated children with a sense of bodily shame and guilt that needs to be overcome.

The C.S.C. (Childhood Sexuality Circle) in California promotes the exchange of information and child pornographic material including tapes, films, and photographs. In addition, many of its reported 10,000 members send one another long, detailed letters describing their victims physically and elaborating on the various sexual activities in which they engage.

N.A.M.B.L.A. (North American Man/Boy Lovers Association) claims to have over 100,000 members although these figures appear to be quite exaggerated. Spokesmen for this group argue that adult society has neither a moral nor legal right to limit a child's selection of sexual partners. They claim that sex with children leads to a healthy orientation toward mature genital satisfaction later in life.**

The British Pedophile Information Exchange (P.I.E.) is advocating that the age of consent for sexual relationships be lowered to four. This group conducts research on pedophilia and actively seeks to change laws, mores and attitudes.***

---

* *AWAKE!* June 22, 1982, p. 5.

** Flyer, North American Man/Boy Lovers Association, P.O. Box 2, Village Station, New York, NY 10014, 1979.

*** Release, P.I.E., 1 Elgin Avenue, London, England, 1979.

Despite these claims to the contrary, all evidence suggests that child sexual abuse has devastating effects on its victims. Children are not capable of consenting relationships, and thus become prey to adults they have been taught to trust by a society that educates its young to obey its elders. The effects of sexual abuse are primarily emotional, leading to dysfunctional behavior that can persist for a lifetime.

## Causes of Sexual Abuse of Children

The causes of incest and pedophilic activities are varied. They are also complicated and distinctive from one another. (See Table 1-1.)

### Incest

Incestuous activities tend to be inter- and intra-generational; i.e., incest occurs between and within different generations. A woman molested as a child by her older brothers may marry a man who, as a child, was molested by a relative. He, in turn, may molest his own children. What often results in an incestuous relationship is a marriage involving a *folie a deux* where neither partner is to blame but where each has sought need satisfaction in dysfunctional ways. Just as the female may be drawn to an ineffectual man, the weak male, in turn, seeks a dominant mother figure. In some instances, women with difficulties achieving mature emotional and genital satisfaction with an adult male may seek partners who also suffer from sexual dysfunction. In other cases, men with unresolved needs for nurturance, and resultant unconscious anger, displace anger onto helpless victims while simultaneously seeking affection from their daughters.

Incest is not linked to social class, to urban or rural populations or to ethnic groups. In other words, incest occurs among all social classes, in cities and in the country, and among all religious and ethnic populations. It should be mentioned that although there is

# Table 1-1: Models: Causes of Sexual Offenses Against Children

**Pedophilia**                                                              **Incest**

### Cultural Factors

- Societal preoccupation with sexuality/sexual prowess (Media stresses importance of sexuality)
- Dynamics of power (Control and power prevail)
- Unacceptability of anger (Outlets for expression of anger are minimal)
- Changes in social structure (Mobility, alienation, rootlessness result in high unemployment, divorce, employed women—leading to less protected children)
- Changes in childrearing (Permissiveness, lack of controls give children freedom)
- Children as objects (Children are viewed as possessions without rights)
- Legal injustices, inconsistencies, ineptitudes (Offenders are not caught, prosecuted, convicted)

### Psychological Factors

| Pedophilia | (center) | Incest |
|---|---|---|
| • Fixation on children | • Early childhood traumatization (abuse, neglect)<br>• Addictive, dependent personality | • Regression to earlier modes of (fantasized) pleasure |
| • Regarding children as emotional, social, physical equals | • Depressive syndrome<br>• Low self-esteem<br>• Repressed anger<br>• Character disorder (low frustration tolerance, poor impulse control, need for immediate gratification, impaired ability to experience guilt, empathy, remorse) | • Sexual orientation within the family |
| • Sexual outlet primarily outside nuclear constellation | | |

### Precipitating Stresses

| Pedophilia | (center) | Incest |
|---|---|---|
| • Loneliness and alienation<br>• Interpersonal isolation | • Poor communication skills<br>• Social isolation<br>• Environmental problems, i.e., unemployment etc. | • Sexual dysfunction<br>• Effects of chemical abuse<br>• Marital discord |

no corroborative data, some authorities believe that incest may occur slightly more frequently among lower socio-economic groups due to financial and social stresses and overcrowding. However, other experts believe that these figures merely indicate that incest tends to be disclosed more among these groups due to their involvement with social service and public welfare agencies.

Certain personality types appear to be at high risk for incestuous relationships. These types include men who have low impulse control, low frustration tolerance, frustrated dependency needs, low self-esteem and a need for immediate gratification of their desires. Often there is early unresolved trauma due to sexual molestation in their backgrounds. They tend to marry young into marriages of long duration. Generally there is an absence of extra-marital affairs in the family.

Social and situational factors contribute strongly to the onset of incest. Dysfunctional relationships, sexual problems, stress and social isolation are among these factors. In other words, incestuous families tend to be multi-problem families.* Alcohol abuse definitely is a contributory factor in a large percentage of cases but it is probably not causative. For example, a number of offenders abuse alcohol at the time that molestation occurs but alcohol alone does not cause them to commit incestuous acts. It simply lowers inhibitions sufficiently to encourage already desired activities.

In one group therapy session involving ten incestuous offenders, participants were asked why they had molested their daughters and stepdaughters. One offender replied, "It's a disease. It's been in my family for over 50 years." Among the other

---

* In 1969, Bagley analyzed a sample of cases of intrafamilial molestation. Five distinct family types emerged from his analysis: 1) functional families with emotionally weak mothers where the daughters assume spousal roles, 2) disorganized families where roles and boundaries are confused and blurred, 3) psychotic families with the presence of severe pathology in one or more parents, 4) pedophilic families with the presence of a fixed, compulsive pedophile as parent, and 5) sociopathic families where the perpetrator is diagnosed as an antisocial personality. In: Bagley, C. "Incest Behavior and Incest Taboo," *Social Problems*, 16, 1969, 505-19.

offenders, other rationalizations abounded. However, once the impasse of denial was broken, most of the participants believed that their behavior was motivated by three factors: anger, power and desire. Several of the men admitted that they molested their daughters simply because they wanted to and chose to act on their desires. Others said that they felt angry and powerless. These men unconsciously chose to displace that anger on helpless children over whom they felt control.

## Pedophilia

Authorities believe that approximately 80%* of pedophiles were themselves molested as children. Pedophilic acts often appear to provide these men with reassurance of their masculinity and give them a sense of power over helpless victims. Some pedophiles are compulsively and repetitively reenacting the trauma of early molestation. Many of these men appear to be fixated at the age when they were molested, i.e., if they were molested at eight or nine, their emotional and psychological growth remains stunted and they tend to have sexual preferences for boys or girls of the same age.

In some cases, pedophiles molested as children identify with the perpetrator or aggressor so that in later life they too become child molesters. In other cases, displaced anger is operating. For example, a boy molested at ten by a pedophile later displaces the anger he felt toward the perpetrator onto small children whom he sexually abuses.

About 20% of known pedophiles do not report having been molested as children. However, there is some data supporting the fact that these individuals were traumatized at an early age and that the age of their young victims coincides with the age at which they were traumatized. The traumatic experience may not have

---

* Groth, A. N. *Men Who Rape: The Psychology of the Offender*. New York: Plenum Press, 1978.

been a single event but may instead have been related to deprivation of early human needs for nurturance and security.

Typically, the pedophile is lonely and isolated, feeling little consolation in adult companionship and little desire to seek out peers for social interactions. Often, these men are intensely uncomfortable and shy with adults. As with incest, however, there is no correlation between pedophilic activities and socio-economic class, occupation, geographic area or ethnic groups. A pedophile may be a physician or a sanitation worker.

High risk victims of pedophiles tend to be young boys or girls who are unsupervised and whose whereabouts during the day or evening are not known for hours at a time. One youngster who frequented a local gym twice weekly would disappear from the premises for twenty to thirty minutes at a time. After several months, authorities learned that the boy was spending that time in a motor home parked near the gym. Apparently no one questioned the fact that this ten-year-old boy returned home with small gifts and money.

## Profile of the Incestuous Triad

With pedophilia, it is possible to discuss the offender without reference to the victim's family since the offense is extrafamilial. Incestuous abuse differs from pedophilia in that the offense occurs within the family. Thus, it is inaccurate and misleading to refer to the offender in isolation. Family dynamics must be considered.

Families in which incest occurs often are referred to as enmeshed. *Enmeshment* is a term used to describe extreme interdependence and involvement among family members. Often there are few social outlets in the homes where incest occurs and guilt regarding socially unacceptable behavior further increases social isolation.

The literature presents a stereotypic picture of the incestuous triad, which typically is composed of mother, daughter and father/stepfather. In some of the literature, the mother is described as an unconscious participant in the "conspiracy of silence." This means that on some level the mother knows that incest is occurring and uses the defense mechanism of denial to block the reality of the family's situation.

Sometimes the mother covertly encourages incestuous abuse by setting up her daughter to be a victim of the father. Motivations for such a mother's behavior vary. She may have been a victim of incest and, due to unresolved anger, unconsciously wants her daughters to encounter the same abuse. On other occasions, a mother who wants to avoid sexual contact with her spouse subtly encourages her daughter to become a surrogate sexual partner for the father.

Mothers in incestuous families typically have been described as passive, dependent, immature and bound to their own mothers. They are seen as rejecting of their daughters. Often they have backgrounds involving emotional deprivation with accompanying anxieties related to fear of desertion. Hence, they fear family disintegration and are highly invested in keeping the family intact.

Although the foregoing generalizations are applicable to many incestuous families, and although almost every incestuous triad is complicated by interdependent dynamics and role reversals, stereotyping of any kind must be avoided. There are many situations in which incest has existed in families where the mothers were not aware, on any level, of its occurrence.

Fathers involved in incestuous relationships are not stereotyped in any one way. Instead, they are variously described as mentally defective, alcoholic, psychotic and psychopathic. A 1984 study of ten incestuous fathers compared with a control group of ten nonincestuous fathers was conducted by Karen Kirland and Chris Bauer, psychologists at the University of Colorado (*Psychology Today*, April, 1984).* Both groups were administered the *MMPI*

---

* Levenson, R. L. "Incestuous Fathers." *Psychology Today*, April, 1984, p. 14.

*(Minnesota Multiphasic Personality Inventory)* which measures different personality traits. Incestuous fathers scored abnormally high on three of the subscales: psychopathic deviate (lack of guilt and remorse), psychasthenia (fears, phobias and compulsions), and schizophrenia. High scorers on these scales often worry about their masculinity, have low impulse control and are socially isolated.

Alcoholism is associated with incest. Some studies indicate that over 75% of incest offenders are alcoholic and/or otherwise chemically dependent. However, alcohol is a contributory and not a causative factor in incestuous abuse. Alcohol decreases inhibitions, thus allowing the drinker to act on impulse. For therapeutic purposes, it is important for professionals to realize the part alcohol often plays in incest. The incestuous father who abuses his child only when drinking or drunk should be referred for treatment of alcoholism, drug abuse or both as part of his overall therapy program.

Some incestuous fathers are mentally defective and some are psychotic. A number of these men are severely antisocial. For this population, treatment goals are limited and the prognosis remains guarded. A client who has no capacity to feel empathy, who objectifies relationships and experiences neither guilt nor remorse, is a poor candidate for therapeutic interventions.

Again, however, stereotyping should be avoided. Many incestuous fathers are treatable. Some are men who experienced stress as children and who revert to earlier modes of (fantasized) satisfaction when they abuse their own children. For others, early conflicts are reactivated during periods of high marital, vocational or financial stress, and they relive unresolved trauma by molesting their own children.

Several studies indicate that the typical incestuous father is fairly rigid and controlling within the family, but maintains limited contact with an outside world in which his behavior is inhibited and nonassertive. He is often found to have been married for some time, to be experiencing sexual incompatibility with his wife, but not to have sought extra-marital affairs. He may also have a sporadic job history. Many do feel guilt regarding incest and this is one reason offenders characteristically deny their acts.

As with pedophiles and sex offenders in general, incestuous males often have a history of sexual abuse.* In one incest offenders therapy group from the Phoenix metropolitan area in 1982, over 70% of the males had experienced childhood incestuous abuse by fathers, mothers or older male and female siblings. Seventy-five percent of the 150 men in the ROARE program in a New Jersey prison were sexually abused as children. All of the 150 men are imprisoned for sexual offenses.**

The incestuous male's chosen victim is highly valued and becomes a surrogate sexual partner for him. Such men, in fact, often seek emotional rather than sexual satisfaction from their daughters. Hence, incest has been described as "intimacy gone wrong." One offender stated that he molested his daughter in an attempt to find "comfort."

For the offender, denial appears to take many forms. Some offenders will claim that they did not abuse their victims, while others rationalize their actions. Excuses vary from "I thought she was my wife" to "She asked for it." Even when an offender admits incestuous abuse, he tends to minimize the degree, extent or possible effects of his actions. There are several reasons for this strong denial. The antisocial personality fears imprisonment. Furthermore, he may not feel that his behavior was morally or ethically wrong. For the majority of incest offenders, however, there appears to be a mixture of guilt and fear—fear of rejection by their partners, fear of family dissolution, fear of incarceration and fear of a general disruption in their lives.

---

* Reported by Nicholas A. Groth of the Connecticut Correctional Institute in Sommerville, "The Silent Shame," NBC Television, August, 1984.

** Foster, J. D. *Suffer the Little Children*. Portsmouth, OH: Keystone Copy Cat. Printing, 1981, p. 18.

Therapists who have treated incestuous offenders sometimes liken them to alcoholics. Both share a compulsion (whether fixed or not); both need confrontation, supportive interventions and monitoring; and both deny or rationalize their behaviors. Before any incest offender is treated, he must be helped to break through the impasse of denial and to fully admit his behaviors.

There is no set personality profile for the victims of incestuous abuse for obvious reasons related to such factors as age, maturity level, mental functioning, and degree of abuse. In addition, we have no data on pre-incest personalities, i.e., we do not know what personality dynamics were operating prior to the abuse.

On the other hand, we do know that victims tend to be distrustful, isolated and secretive. Many are dishonest, self-blaming and lacking in boundaries due to role-reversals in the family. If not helped, their behavior often becomes antisocial—involving lying, stealing, truancy, chemical abuse and sexual promiscuity. Low self-esteem characterizes these girls, whose self-loathing often manifests itself in suicidal attempts and self-mutilation.

The theory of victim precipitation predominated in the literature until recent years. According to this theory, victims literally invited molestation and were characterized as being seductive with their fathers. Along with the theory of victim precipitation was the notion that victims often lied about abuse or exaggerated the extent of the molestation. Authorities in the field now refute the theory of victim precipitation. If children appear to "invite" abuse, it is because they have learned seductive behaviors following molestation. For some girls, molestation is the only type of physical contact they have had with a parent and they literally learn to sexualize all relationships. No child initially invites abuse, nor can any child be held responsible for sexual abuse.

An important therapeutic goal with victims is to help them learn nonseductive behaviors and assertiveness. It is imperative that they be taught self-respect, to say *No* to a molester and to use specific methods for the protection of their own bodies. Victims need to learn that they are not alone; that adult support does exist; that they are not responsible for being abused; and that they should not feel guilty for the abuse sustained. (It is unfortunate that we must teach young children to protect themselves against so-called "trusted" adults, but the realities of our current legal system necessitate this approach.)

Experts also refute the notion that victims lie about sexual abuse. The consensus is that over 99% of girls who claim that they have been sexually abused are telling the truth.* It is important to believe victims since irrevocable psychological harm can result when professionals doubt a child who has built up sufficient courage to disclose molestation to a parent or other authority figure.

A typical example of an enmeshed family involved in incestuous abuse came to attention when a sixteen-year-old female victim was arrested for theft, placed on probation and referred for counseling. The youngster revealed a lengthy history of delinquent acts, school truancy and chemical abuse. She also informed her therapist that her natural father had abused her physically since infancy and had raped her at the age of ten.

The teenager's passive and dependent mother claimed that she had been aware of the beatings her daughter suffered but not of the sexual molestation that continued from the girl's tenth to thirteenth year. The woman stated that she did not realize her daughter was physically abused by the beatings. She believed that all children needed to be punished and although she felt that her husband was too strict, she also realized that he loved his daughter and was "trying to rear her right." However, the daughter had not disclosed that incest was occurring because she felt that her mother either would not believe her or would send her away from home. In therapy, she stated that she had started to date at age

---

* Herman, J. and Hirschman, L. *Father-Daughter Incest.* Cambridge: Harvard University Press, 1980.

thirteen and that her father had then turned his attention to a younger daughter.

In this family, the mother was at home and unemployed. She too had been an early victim of sexual abuse. She had never had a satisfactory emotional or sexual relationship with her spouse, who drank heavily and was periodically unemployed. Unconsciously, this mother may have set the stage for her daughters to become victims of sexual abuse.

When incest finally was disclosed in therapy, the sixteen-year-old girl felt both relief and fear. Child Protective Services was notified to investigate the possibility of current molestation in the home. All members of the family, including the two girls, then denied allegations of current abuse and no action was taken.

## Profile of the Pedophile

Contrary to popular opinion, the pedophile is not necessarily a homosexual. He is a man (or occasionally a woman) who derives primary sexual, emotional and psychological gratification from children. Sometimes he molests a child only once, as did one pedophile who paid several hundred dollars to spend one night with a five-year-old girl, and as did an otherwise exemplary Boy Scout leader who molested one of his charges on an overnight camping trip. More often, however, the pedophile seeks a long-term, loving relationship with a child, as in the case of one who purchased a boy from his parents for the sum of several thousand dollars, or the single adult male who adopted a youngster and subsequently molested him over a period of years. Usually, pedophiles do not pay large sums of money for their victims. Instead, they seduce children with loving attention, physical affection, verbal praise and a wide variety of other rewards.

Almost all pedophiles (about 99%) tend to be passive, lonely men. Only about one percent are sadists who cruelly assault their victims through rape and torture. This one percent is the group that we tend to hear about most often in the media because of the atypical sensationalism associated with their acts.

Pedophiles may be divorced, married, separated or single. The majority of them are men over the age of eighteen. Some incestuous fathers engage in extrafamilial pedophilic acts. In these cases, the fathers are classified as pedophiles because their primary orientation appears to be toward children in general and not just toward their own offspring.

One striking characteristic of the pedophile is his ability to minimize or rationalize his activities. Minimization and rationalization are forms of denial and are characteristic of all sexual offenders including incest offenders and rapists. Often, the pedophile will claim that his behavior is perfectly normal, or he may try to place the blame on the child for seductive behavior. Perhaps this tendency to rationalize relates to a need of the pedophile to minimize or deny the molestation that he himself may have suffered in childhood.

A second important trait of the pedophile relates directly to denial. The majority of pedophiles are characterized by an inability to experience guilt or remorse regarding their actions. Denial can result from the fact that the pedophile truly does not feel that his behavior has a deleterious effect on the victim. Even if he were convinced that he had harmed the child, he might be incapable of caring. The pedophile usually lacks a social conscience. Lack of guilt and remorse characterize the antisocial personality (the socio- or psychopathic personality). Generally, this personality type objectifies others, i.e., treats people as objects to be used and manipulated for his own ends. Relationships tend to be transitory and shallow, and social norms are respected only superficially. Responsible behavior in the work, home or social setting is distinctly lacking. Antisocial personalities have low impulse control and low frustration tolerance, and they comprise the majority of our criminal population.

A. Nicholas Groth, a leading authority on offenders and the author of *Men Who Rape: The Psychology of the Offender*, believes that there are two categories of pedophiles—regressed and fixated.

## Regressed Pedophile

The regressed pedophile tends to revert to an early mode of (fantasized) behavior, satisfaction and/or gratification when he is under stress. Because his behavior is neither habitual nor compulsive, he tends to be more amenable to therapeutic interventions.

An example of a regressed pedophile is a man who may be experiencing extreme stress in his life. This man has lost his job and fights constantly with his wife. Under stress, he suddenly feels quite powerless and angry. His masculinity and sense of adult identity are threatened. Needs for affection and nurturance have been thwarted due to marital strain. Under these conditions, the man may turn to a child to meet his emotional needs or to express his anger. This pattern of behavior is much more typical of incestuous offenders than of pedophiles, but there appear to be cases where pedophilia is neither a compulsive nor a habitual pattern.

One 50-year-old man, forced into early retirement by a back injury, developed high blood pressure and diabetes. Relations between this man and his wife were severely strained, and he became impotent for the first time in their 25-year marriage. Within six months from the date of his retirement, this man was arrested for molesting a six-year-old neighborhood girl. The molestation appears to have been motivated primarily by a need to assert manhood and, secondarily, served as an expression of anger related to declining masculine prowess and illness.

In another instance, a teenage boy of eighteen (who had been molested at four by an older cousin) sexually abused a five-year-old boy on one occasion behind a store. The precipitating cause of the molestation was traced to extreme frustration over failing school grades and family stress intensified when a married sister and her children moved back to the boy's home. Unconsciously, this youngster was displacing anger over the molestation he had suffered onto another child at a time of great stress and frustration.

## Fixated Pedophile

Unlike the regressed pedophile, the fixated pedophile is emotionally and psychologically ''stuck'' at an early age, often at the age when he was molested. Every week the newspapers report stories about men from ages 18 to 80 who have been arrested for sexually assaulting children. Their police records often reveal histories of years of multiple assaults. These men have a fixed, habitual compulsion to molest children of a certain age, comparable in some ways to the compulsion that alcoholics have to drink. The prognosis for successful treatment of this type of pedophile, the most common type, is extremely poor.

A recent headline in the *Arizona Republic* reads, '' 'Cured' Molester Admits 57 New Counts.'' The story recounted details of the sexual activities of a 42-year-old pedophile who had appeared on the CBS-TV program ''60 Minutes'' in 1978 to tell how he had been cured of child molesting. During his 1983 trial, he was charged with 57 new counts of lewd and lascivious behavior with over a dozen boys. He faced 133 years to life in prison for the felony charges of child molesting including oral copulation and sodomy between 1981-1983. This man's record of sexual offenses dated back to 1964 and he had been sent to Atascadero State Hospital in California several times for psychiatric help. His victims, ages eight to fourteen, were seduced with toys, games and money and then were taken on weekend trips for sexual activities.

## Mysopedic Behavior

There is a third type of pedophile, uncommon but still meriting attention because of the sadistic and lethal nature of his activities.

He is the vicious child rapist, sometimes involved in sado-masochistic cults, who often mutilates and murders his victims, sometimes in ritualistic fashion. The term for this child hater is "mysoped" and his behavior is referred to as "mysopedic."*

Several years ago in California a registered MDSO (mentally disordered sex offender) was arrested for the brutal rape and murder of a two-and-one-half-year-old girl he had abducted from her home. This man had a lengthy history of sadistic molestation of children. He had been arrested seventeen times, with three convictions for sexually assaulting young children. Just prior to the murder of the two-and-one-half-year-old girl, he had been released as cured from the sexual offenders' treatment program at Atascadero State Hospital. Clearly, this man is a mysoped; his behavior is not amenable to therapeutic interventions. The little girl's grandmother began a program called S.L.A.M. (Society's League Against Molesters) which now has a number of chapters nationwide.

Another example of a mysoped is Pogo the Clown, who entertained children in hospitals and in his home in suburban Illinois. When Pogo was finally arrested for a sex crime, police found piles of skeletal remains in his home. He stated that he had sexually assaulted and strangled 32 teenage boys and young men, then buried their remains in his home or dumped them in a nearby river.

There are several types of regressed and fixated pedophiles. The "Chicken Hawk" is the adult male who seduces teenage boys between the ages of thirteen and eighteen. Victims are referred to as "chickens." The heterosexual pedophile is the adult male (or female) who seduces girls (or boys) from infancy to puberty, but usually between ages four and twelve. Bisexual pedophiles also

* One hundred fifty thousand to two hundred thousand children disappear each year (three to four thousand per week). Two-thirds of these children are abducted by estranged parents. The rest are taken by strangers or die in accidents. Of those taken by strangers, eighty percent or forty thousand, are never found. Ten percent (three thousand) are found murdered and another ten percent are returned to their parents. (Editors, *Missing*, Peer Group Communications Corporation, New York, NY, Vol. 1, #1, January, 1984).

seduce children from infancy to just beyond puberty. The homosexual male pedophile is attracted to boys who usually are six to nine, or nine to twelve years of age. In other words, a male homosexual pedophile attracted to eleven-year-old boys is not interested in seven-year-old girls.

The victims of pedophiles are referred to by various names such as "kittens" or "angels" (for girls) and "puppies" or "chickens" (for boys). In general, pedophiles abuse pre-pubescent children. The youngest known victim, according to Jill Haddad, a national expert on the subject and co-author of *We Have A Secret*, was two-and-one-half hours old.

High risk pedophiles appear to be unmarried males over the age of eighteen who relate better to children than to adults because they are emotionally fixated at the ages of nine, ten, or eleven. They tend to seek employment in child care centers as teachers or counselors. They are scout leaders, Big Brothers and volunteers with boys' clubs. These men frequent arcades, bike shops, stores that remain open all night, bowling alleys, bus stops, schools, parks, beaches, amusement centers, swap meets, theaters, and markets. Despite this high risk profile, it is important to remember that pedophiles can be of any age, married or single, bisexual, homosexual or heterosexual. They work in such varied occupations as laborer, social worker, physician, computer sales manager, bank official—any job that can be named.

The knowledge we currently have regarding offenders is useful to the clinician interested in careful assessment and evaluation. However, we must deepen and refine that knowledge through research studies focusing both on etiology and treatment if we hope to combat the growing problem of child sexual abuse.

# 2

# Understanding Approaches and Patterns of Offenders

The professional community has been slow to recognize the differences between incest offenders and pedophiles. The lay community still views sexual offenders of different types as a homogenous group of perverts. In order to refine and improve methods of prevention and treatment interventions, professionals must learn to distinguish and differentiate among all types of sexual offenders, their motivations and methods of seduction, as well as learn how to identify high-risk victims.

## Patterns of Incestuous Abuse

The majority of incest offenders (97-99%) are male, and the majority of victims (92-95%) are female.* The most commonly reported form of incestuous abuse involves a father with a daughter

---

* Herman, J. and Hirschman, L. ''Father-Daughter Incest.'' In: Schultz, L.G.(ed.) *The Sexual Victimology of Youth*. Springfield, IL: Charles C. Thomas, Publisher, 1980, p. 98.

or a father with his stepdaughter. Mother-son or mother-daughter abuse appears to be quite rare and when it does occur, the consequences can be disastrous, sometimes resulting in personality disintegration or psychosis for victims.

Grandfather-granddaughter molestation is common, along with uncle-niece and brother-sister abuse. If the grandfather is close to the father's age, the dynamics are similar to father-daughter incest. If the grandfather is much older, he appears to be motivated by a need to reassert his masculinity. Brother-sister incest can be relatively harmless if the siblings are close in age and involved in mutual sex play or sex exploration. If, however, the brother is much older or more powerful than his sister, the consequences to the victim can be serious.

Usually incest begins with fondling when the victim is five to seven years of age, although abuse can start either earlier or when the child is older. Typically, the victims are the eldest female children in the family. Fondling continues and can progress to full intercourse when the victim is pubescent.

Incest is a family secret. Child victims sense that "something is wrong" but they trust their parents and other adults in the family both as caretakers and authority figures. The offender misuses this trust, hoping that the child will not disclose incest; and typically girls do not tell anyone until they are thirteen or fourteen years of age.

There are several reasons why a teenager eventually does disclose incest. At thirteen, she may want to expand her social life and begins to resent the limits imposed on her by her offender. Hence, she discloses her "secret" to her mother, a school counselor, a friend or relative. She may fear pregnancy, or become jealous if her offender begins to express an interest in a younger sibling.

Generally, incestuous offenders do not physically mistreat their victims even though they may threaten them. The youngsters appear to remain silent because of fear and guilt. They are afraid that their mothers may not believe them if they say that incest is occurring, or that their father, uncle or grandfather may carry through with threats, or that disclosure might result in dissolution of the family. In addition, they are likely to feel guilty because they deeply believe that something is wrong with them, something that resulted in their being sexually molested. Like battered wives and physically abused children, victims of sexual abuse internalize guilt and blame themselves for being victimized.

## Methods and Approaches of Seduction for Pedophiles

Unlike the incest offender, the pedophile does not live within the home. Consequently, children may not be readily available to him. Hence, his entire approach to his victim is different from that of the incest offender. Unfortunately, the public has a stereotypic concept of the pedophile, who, in reality, is not a conspicuous deviant wearing a trench coat and hat. He is not "Mr. Stranger Danger."

Ninety percent of pedophiles are friendly and many of them are known to the families of the victims. The pedophile's approach usually involves befriending and establishing trust with the child and his family. The seduction may take weeks or even months. Often, the pedophile becomes a "pal" to the child by developing a slow, caring relationship and by paying more attention to the child than his parent does.

The pedophile's attitude toward the child is protective and concerned as he offers gifts, trips to arcades and ball parks and weekend boating or fishing expeditions. He pursues the child with eye contact, furtive glances and stares centered on the genital area. Eventually, to stimulate the child and lower inhibitions, he may introduce his intended victim to drugs or alcohol or both. The child also may be introduced to pornographic literature in order to further lower inhibitions and to relieve the intended victim of any guilt associated with deviant activities.

The offender usually photographs the child, either to introduce him or her to the business of pornography or to keep a permanent record of the relationship—which, of necessity, is short-term. As the child reaches adolescence, the pedophile loses sexual interest and the photographs serve as a permanent reminder of the transient relationship.

Some pedophiles do not have easy access to children and resort to seeking out pimps to find child prostitutes. Child prostitutes usually are boys of fourteen or fifteen who have run away from home and who earn $20.00 to $40.00 "a trick," or $25.00 to $1,000 per day. These boys are asked to watch porno flicks, take drugs or drink, and agree to be photographed. Later, these children may become pimps when they are too old to be attractive to pedophiles. The child prostitution market is extensive and child sex rings to promote prostitution abound in many cities in this country. Boys' homes, private schools and boys' clubs often are fronts for these rings, which are run by "Chicken Hawks" and pedophiles of all types.

Child prostitution is closely linked to the pornography market. Ninety percent of the publications featuring children are purchased by mail order. The titles of these magazines aptly describe their contents: *Lollitots, Boys Who Love Boys, Children Love, and How to Pick Up Little Girls: A Child's Lover's Guide to Better Child Loving. Where the Young Ones Are*, by Daniel M. Yert, lists 378 places in 59 cities of 34 states where young child victims can be located. This 1972 publication sold 70,000 copies in a little over a year from the date of publication.

Sometimes nude photographs of children depicted in the various magazines are quite explicit, showing children engaging in various sexual activities together, or showing adults sexually involved with children. Other photographs depict nude children in harmless, natural poses. All such pictures are enticing and stimulating to the pedophile.

However, commercial magazines, films and slides constitute only about ten percent of the child pornography market, despite the fact that pornographic magazines easily retail for between $7.50 and $12.50. Most pornograhy is made by pedophiles for private use and for sharing with peers.

## Illustrative Case Histories

A case study involving a nine-year-old boy living with his divorced mother and her boyfriend will help illustrate what may happen when a youngster becomes involved with a pedophile. This child's natural father, who had physically abused Mark as a baby, lived out of state. He was an intelligent youngster who performed well in school and appeared to be fairly well adjusted at home.

> *One day, Mark began to come home late from school, claiming that he was stopping off to play a few video games at the local arcade. As time passed, he spent more and more time away from home, often returning from school as late as 7:00 or 8:00 p.m.*
>
> *There were some subtle behavioral changes in the boy. He appeared to withdraw from contacts with his friends and occasionally had money, of unexplained origin, in his possession. At home, he appeared irritable and preoccupied. The boy seemed particularly defensive about his activities and it did occur to his mother that he might be engaging in petty shoplifting. Mark's interest in school seemed to wane.*
>
> *On the day Mark returned home at 10:00 p.m. with no logical explanation of his whereabouts, his mother decided to investigate. She spoke to the manager of the local arcade, who advised her that Mark often did stop by to play a game or two after school, but that he always left within an hour*

*or so. Mark's mother then sought counseling for the youngster, who finally admitted that he had met a man at the arcade some months before and that for the past two months he had been involved in pedophilic activities..*

Several important issues arise from this case summary. The mother clearly was remiss in not questioning her nine-year-old son's activities earlier. She did not pay sufficient attention to numerous secondary cues, such as unexplained money the youngster had in his possession, a change from outgoing to withdrawn behavior, preoccupied and defensive behavior, and a marked change in patterns of activity.

A second case history will further illustrate pedophilic behavior and the variations that can occur in interactions.

*Marny was a lonely, unattractive divorced woman of 33. She had two sons in her custody, Billy, aged six, and Bobby, aged eleven. Jim, a single, attractive 28-year-old man, lived in the same apartment complex as Marny and her sons.*

*Since Marny worked until five p.m., her boys remained unsupervised each day between the hours of 2:30 and 5:30 p.m. During those hours, the youngsters watched TV, had friends visit the home, or played ball on the street.*

*Gradually, Jim (who was self-employed and worked at home) began to befriend Billy and Bobby by encouraging them to swim in the apartment complex pool and by playing touch football with them. Little by little, he began to establish trust with the boys who looked forward to seeing him each day. That pattern continued for about a month.*

*One day, Jim stopped by Marny's apartment in the evening and offered to take the family out for dinner. Lonely and flattered by the attention, Marny agreed and the evening was enjoyable for everyone. Thereafter, Jim dated Marny with regularity but the couple did not engage in sexual activities.*

*Two years of pedophilic activity were disclosed when the boys were eight and thirteen and began to act out in the community. The relationship between Jim and Billy and Bobby had involved anal intercourse, fondling and fellatio. The youngsters had engaged in fellatio with one another at Jim's command and both had been photographed on numerous occasions while bathing and having sex with one another. Some of these activities had occurred in the home. Others occurred on camping trips and still others in motel rooms in the city. During those two years, Jim had dated and courted Marny but had never had sexual intercourse with her. Like all pedophiles, he had no more interest in an adult female than a heterosexual has in someone of the same sex. During his court hearing, Jim admitted to molesting six different boys in the preceding fifteen years.*

When we look closely at cases of pedophilia, we see certain patterns emerge. Children of divorce are more vulnerable to the attention of pedophiles. Often, they lack proper supervision and seek male attention. Their mothers are busy working and coping with the general stresses associated with divorce. Sometimes the children are experiencing behavioral, adjustment or learning difficulties that add to their loneliness and need for love and affection. Most often, they are pubescent boys who have more freedom than their female counterparts and who are more desirable to the pedophile seeking his next victim.

A final case history involving an incest offender highlights the differences between extrafamilial and intrafamilial molestation.

> *Warren, aged 35, married Jean, a dominant woman, when both were in their early twenties. After twelve years of sexual and emotional incompatibility, the couple divorced. Jean was awarded custody of both eleven-year-old Shelly and eight-year-old Tom. Both Warren and Jean remarried. Two summers after the divorce, Warren began to molest Shelly during her weekend visits. Molestation involved fondling and digital penetration. This continued for six months until Shelly disclosed the incestuous behavior to her best friend who, in turn, told her mother.*
>
> *The case was reported to the authorities, and while awaiting court action, Warren voluntarily sought treatment. During therapy, Warren began to understand his feelings of inferiority and sexual inadequacy. To please his wives and "measure up to them," he had felt the need to perform sexually for their benefit with little or no consideration of his own needs. During a stressful period involving a family move, a new job and the death of a relative, Warren's feelings of inadequacy increased and he turned to Shelly for comfort, acceptance and reassurance of his masculinity.*

Warren represents a typical incest offender who regressed during a stressful period. His behavior was neither fixated nor compulsive. Hence, the prognosis was favorable with treatment focusing on self-image building, control issues, stress management and sex therapy for both Warren and his wife.

## Children Who Are At Risk

It is important to become aware of the specific characteristics of high risk victims of sexual abuse. For these children, there are both physical and behavioral indicators for professionals to recognize.

Physical indicators of child sexual abuse include the presence of venereal disease, pregnancy, difficulty with urination, vaginal or penile discharge, lacerations or bruises in the genital area and hematomas. When any of these symptoms is present, sexual abuse should be suspected.

Victims of pedophiles in particular tend to be children of divorce. McKee reports that 80% of the victims of pedophiles come from divorced families.* Boys aged eight to eleven appear to be particularly vulnerable to the advances of the pedophile. These youngsters definitely fall into the high risk category when they are unsupervised for long periods of time, when they run away from home or when they become "missing children." Boys who spend hours at a time at arcades, bike shops, parks, public swimming pools, and convenience stores (or all-night markets) are easy prey to pedophiles.

In addition, youngsters who are experiencing behavioral or adjustment difficulties of any kind appear to be at risk. Children who are lonely and depressed seek affection from any source. Boys who have learning difficulties or handicaps tend to be rejected by their peers and will seek out adult attention. Children with handicaps or deficiencies appear to be ready victims for both pedophiles and incestuous offenders, partly because there is less

---

* McKee, B. *Run-Aways, Throw-Aways*. Scottsdale, AZ: Good-Life Productions, 1980.

likelihood that they will disclose the fact that abuse is occurring. Defiant and angry children may rebel against parental authority and become truants from school or spend hours away from home. These children, too, are easy victims for pedophiles.

One seven-year-old youngster was highly depressed and angry over the recent divorce of his parents and the subsequent indifference expressed by his father. Because he was small for his age and mentally somewhat impaired, he was ignored by children in the neighborhood. When a 55-year-old married man who lived across the street invited him to swim in his pool, the youngster readily accepted without seeking his mother's permission. Within two weeks, trust had been established between this youngster and his adult friend who began photographing him in the nude and fondling him in the swimming pool. The boy reported all of his activities to his mother except for the sexual relationship he was having with this pedophile.

Parents and professionals should be particularly aware of any unexplained changes in children's behavior. Many victims of both incest and pedophilia become provocative, seductive and/or sexually promiscuous. Others show signs of regression by acting childishly, withdrawing into fantasy lives or sucking their thumbs.

A mother who suspects her daughter may be a victim of incest should ask these questons: Why does the girl seem particularly hostile to her parents? Why does she suddenly object to being alone with her father, stepfather or another adult male member of the family? Why does this male: a) seem overly-protective of the girl and/or jealous of her friends? b) go to bed after everyone else, or get up frequently during the night? c) appear preoccupied with the girl's clothing? or d) behave in a hostile manner towards the girl, joking about her physical development? The mother should also take careful action to find out what goes on in the home when she is at work, especially if she works at night.

With reference to pedophilia, parents should be constantly alert to changes in their child's behavior. How has the child's behavior changed recently? Why does the socially active youngster suddenly withdraw from friends? Is the child arriving early or late to school? Where does a young boy obtain clothes or toys that his parents did not purchase? Why does he come home with money after his allowance has been spent? Where did he learn new adult phrases? Is there a defensive quality about his verbal interactions? Does he appear to resent being questioned about his daily activities?

These are the kinds of questions that parents should be asking themselves—and the kinds of questions that should never be rationalized, ignored, or dismissed with easy answers. All too often a parent delays acting by minimizing his or her own concern. Professionals are in a position to encourage parents to ask such questions and alert them to potential dangers of child sexual abuse. Such awareness on the part of parents and others who work with children will greatly improve efforts for prevention and intervention in cases of child sexual abuse.

# 3

# Interviewing Victims and Their Families

Before elaborating on specific interviewing techniques, it is necessary that the child's family be considered. Understanding certain psychological dynamics within a family will enhance the interviewer's ability to meet the needs of the victimized child. Child sexual abuse inevitably precipitates crisis situations for victims and their families. It is therefore advisable for the professional interviewer to be aware of the psychological effects of these crisis situations. He or she also must be aware of certain characteristics of the individuals involved in crises and the goals of crisis counseling so as to be most effective in interviewing the families and victims. (See Table 3-1.)

Psychological crisis often precipitates some confusion and disorganization in the thinking process. It is not uncommon for parents of victims to confuse time sequences, erratically jump from topic to topic and/or propose solutions that are illogical. Behaviorally, a client in crisis may show signs of impulsiveness, impaired ability to function effectively, and dependence upon authority figures.

## Table 3-1: Crisis Intervention
# Counseling Checklist for Sexual Abuse Clients

_____ Clarify professional's role (who professional is, why professional is present).

_____ Attend to immediate needs (physical or emotional trauma).

_____ Build trust and rapport through empathic approach.

_____ Provide verbal reassurances regarding four key issues: (1) victim is correct to report abuse; (2) victim is not responsible/guilty; (3) victim is not alone; and (4) victim is believed.

_____ Determine exact details of what occurred.

_____ Address common themes for victims (anger, shame, guilt and fear) through focusing on feelings.

_____ Help victim to focus on here-and-now issues.

_____ Involve and reassure family; enlist family's support/cooperation.

_____ Assess coping capacities of victim and family.

_____ Ensure safety for victim through directive (short-term) planning for immediate future events.

_____ Notify authorities (police and Child Protective Services).

_____ Provide needed information regarding aftermath; i.e., legal information, also facts about emotional and physical effects of abuse (Refer to other professionals if necessary).

_____ Help parents to use social network (friends, school nurse, clergy, crisis centers, counseling agencies) through direct referral.

_____ Provide for follow-up contact.

At the same time, largely because of their feelings of dependence, the parents might feel hostile toward authorities. This hostility is a form of displacement, i.e., the parents are actually angry at themselves—due to guilt, dependence, and feelings of vulnerability and helplessness; or they may harbor suppressed rage at the relative or pedophile for the offense committed.

The interviewer should be aware of all of these characteristics, along with typical reactions of people under stress, and the effects of extreme stress. Some people either find the resources to deal with current stressful situations, or are able to emotionally and/or physically escape from these situations. Others become quite combative and tend to react aggressively. Stress takes its toll, however, and in the aftermath of a crisis, the family's coping abilities often diminish. For example: in August, 1981, a three-year-old female child was abducted from her parents who were vacationing in a resort town in California. The parents coped quite well with the crisis and the child was returned within ten days, apparently unharmed physically but damaged psychologically. Two months after the girl's return the parents were experiencing difficulties coping with feelings regarding the abduction and they sought therapy for themselves. Initially this family coped well but the aftermath of the stressful situation left them vulnerable and in need of help.

## The Role of the Interviewer

People in crisis often need concrete guidance and direction. It is important when interviewing family members to establish rapport quickly by assuming a caring, supportive, reassuring posture. Avoid judgements and do not react negatively to displaced hostility. Hostility is best handled by allowing for ventilation. Do not confront and do not personalize issues. In general, help the family to focus on the current situation. Do this by:

- Talking to members separately

- Using open-ended questions

- Identifying, clarifying, labeling and restating facts and feelings

Do not take sides. Simply show a desire to help. Be assertive and clear regarding your recommendations.

Keeping the goals of the interview in mind helps the professional monitor her or his own conduct. The interviewer wants:

- To find out what happened

- To assess the coping style of the parents (in order to be certain that the child will be safe and that the parents will follow through with appropriate actions

- To provide a sense of the interviewer's willingness to help

- To provide reassurance

- To decide what action needs to be taken

The following excerpt from an interview between a medical social worker and the mother of a male victim of pedophilia may illustrate this point:

**Mother**: *I just want him locked up. I can't believe this happened.*

**Social Worker**: *I understand your frustration and the shock you are feeling.* (Clarifying feelings)

**Mother**: *Will Jeff be all right? Do you think permanent damage was done to him? Will he be queer?*

**Social Worker**: *Jeff needs to talk about what happened to him. It may take him a while to open up and he probably will need to see a professional. Be patient. Don't imagine the worst for him. Take it one step at a time.* (Giving subtle direction while helping the client to remain calm)

**Mother**: *I don't know how to act with him. All I can think about is what happened.*

**Social Worker**: *Be yourself. But don't judge or pry. Above all, don't blame Jeff. He wasn't responsible. It wasn't his fault.* (Giving advice and direction)

In the above illustration the social worker understands that the mother is not ready emotionally to deal with specific questions regarding particulars of the molestation. Gradually, the social worker will continue to build trust. She will determine the mother's coping style and support system and how she feels about talking to the police. The important point is that the caring social worker does not confront. She is patient and sensitive to her client's feelings.

# Interviewing the Victim

For several reasons, interviewing child victims is often extremely difficult. Feeling frightened and guilty, the child may be (understandably) either withdrawn or defensive. He or she may be angry at the offender, but probably unaware of this anger. Usually, the youngster's feelings toward the offender are mixed. This is because offenders usually treat their victims well in order to win their love. Sometimes, sexual touching is the only form of affection a child victim has ever known.

Since victims should be interviewed in a quiet location, devoid of connotations of sexual activity, the home or car are not appropriate locations for interviews. The professional should be attentive, honest and patient. Shock and anger should never be expressed. Nor is it advisable to take sides or to judge the offender. Understand the needs of the child; openly express caring feelings, warmth and empathy; but remain emotionally calm.

It is important that verbal and nonverbal behaviors match. Kind words will fall on deaf ears if the interviewer expresses shock or anger nonverbally. It is desirable for the interviewer to maintain eye contact and sit near the child without the barrier of a desk between them.

Above all else, the interviewer should consider three things:

1. The chronological and developmental age of the child

2. The victim's level of sophistication and maturity

3. The current degree of traumatization

In order to build rapport and to assess the child's emotional and mental state, the interviewer needs to first ask general questions regarding school, home life, friends and activities. The use of drawings often aids in this assessment and helps to establish rapport with children.

With older children, interviewers can expect resistance stemming from fear, embarrassment, guilt and/or loyalty to the offender. Above all, maintain a professional stance; neither over-identify with the child nor become his or her rescuer. The interviewer should understand his or her personal values and place them in abeyance. It requires a high degree of self-knowledge to maintain objectivity and balance.

At the outset, assure the child that he or she is blameless and that disclosing facts to the interviewer is right and necessary for the child's own protection. Specific information related to the molestation should be obtained whenever possible. What acts were committed? What inducements were used? Were there any other victims? Were there any other adults present? Were photographs taken? Find out specific locations and times related to the abuse. Do not, however, belabor issues, or press the child for lengthy explanations. Use the language of the child and neither coach nor supply answers. Be permissive and allow for ventilation. Ask open-ended questions requiring more than a yes or no response. Rather than attributing emotions to the child, generalize your comments: for example, instead of saying "You must have felt very guilty," say "That might make some children feel guilty."

When discussing sex, be explicit in order not to convey shame or discomfort. Many hospitals, police departments and counseling centers have purchased anatomically correct dolls for use with young child victims during investigations and court hearings. The children are allowed to play freely with the dolls and to undress and re-dress them at will. The interviewer may ask the child to identify different parts of the body (hands, legs, etcetera). It is best to allow the victim to use his or her own language. Sometimes the child spontaneously reenacts the abusive situation. If the child does not undress a doll, the interviewer may assist by unfastening the doll's shirt and asking the child to identify body parts hidden by clothing.

If the child does not volunteer information, the child may be asked to describe what happened, encouraging use of the dolls to act out the abuse. The therapist might ask, "Can you show me what happened by using the dolls?" "When did that happen?" "Did anything else happen?" "Show me." It is often helpful to make a videotape or audiotape of the session for possible court use.

Child victims are entitled to know about any legal action that will be taken. Partly to relieve the victim's anxiety, and partly to validate the interviewer's trustworthiness, the child should be informed of what is to happen. Answer questions in simple words without volunteering unnecessary information such as the probability of long, worrisome delays in a possible court process.

Children should, however, be told that any incident of molestation must be reported and that they will be required to talk to the authorities about what happened to them. Assure them of your ongoing support.

At some point during the therapeutic process, victims of all forms of sexual abuse need to be reassured on the following points:

1.  Sexual abuse happens to thousands of children every year; they are not alone.

2.  No matter how they behaved or what they did, they are not responsible in any way for the abuse that occurred in their lives. *Always*, adults are responsible for what they do to children.

3.  Sexual abuse is against the law and any adult who abuses a child is breaking the law.

4.  No matter what they did or how they felt (even if they sometimes enjoyed being touched or fondled sexually) they should not feel guilty. Our bodies can respond even when our minds tell us that we do not like what is happening. The fact is that they have done nothing wrong. The adult was wrong.

5.  They may feel afraid but they must learn that there are people who can help them—even if they have been threatened and told not to say anything to anyone.

6.  They need to know and remember that they did the right thing by telling someone. If their parent or friend is punished or if their family now experiences some difficulties, it is not their fault.

## Interviewing Parents

Anyone who is called upon to interview the parents of child victims of sexual abuse can expect to encounter a wide variety of emotional reactions including grief, fear, sorrow, anger, guilt and shock. Elizabeth Kubler-Ross, an authority on the subject of death and dying, recounts the stages that terminally ill patients pass through from the moment they learn that they are dying until they reach a time of acceptance or resolution. These stages are applicable to any serious, stressful or crisis event, and help to explain the emotional state of parents of victims of pedophilia or incest.

First, the parent(s) may experience a need for immediate denial that molestation has occurred. Denial is usually followed by anger. The parent asks, "Why has this happened to my child?" There may be a period of bargaining where the parent silently says, "If only this hadn't happened! I will be a perfect parent from now on!" Denial, anger and bargaining are then followed by a period of depression and grief. Finally, there is an acceptance of the reality of the situation. These stages are not invariably sequential; i.e., a parent may be angry at one moment and then depressed the next.

The first prerequisite for interviewing is to understand the emotional state of the client or parent who has just learned that his or her child has been sexually abused. Feelings of denial, anger, depression and bargaining usually compound and complicate equally strong emotions related to guilt and sorrow. Parents naturally feel responsible. They ask themselves how molestation could have happened without their knowledge and why they didn't notice clues.

Some parents are so emotionally disturbed that they will project blame on the child in order to alleviate their own sense of inadequacy and guilt. Other parents are angry at their children for not having disclosed the abuse at an earlier time. These parents can be quite difficult to interview. It is essential, however, that they be allowed to ventilate their feelings of projection onto the interviewer and not onto the child who can suffer irreparable damage if she or he becomes the object of parental blame or recrimination.

One eight-year-old boy had had a twenty-year-old male babysitter for several months. The young man, a college student known to the family, appeared to be completely trustworthy. One Christmas morning when the family awoke and was ready to open their gifts, the parents realized that their youngest son was not present. The father went next door to see if his son was visiting the babysitter. The child answered the door and the father saw the babysitter emerging from the bedroom, zipping his pants.

The father knew immediately what had happened. He became enraged, accusing both his son and the young man of despicable acts. He cast blame upon the boy and threatened to take him to court for delinquent behavior. Unfortunately, the psychological harm this parent inflicted upon his child may have been far worse than the act of the babysitter. A desirable prognosis was made more difficult. What must be understood is that all responding adults, whether they be parents, interviewers, or others, have a key role in determining the prognoses of sexually abused children.

Conditions for parental interviews, like those for talking to child victims, must be free from distractions and provide a comfortable, neutral location. Again, do not express shock, disapproval or anger. Avoid a judgmental attitude. Professionals should not project their own feelings onto parents. Maintain a neutral stance and explain why information is needed. Obtain the names of people the child has been with, the dates and the locations. Assess how the parents deal with crises and what support systems are present in their lives.

Effective interviewing techniques with individuals in a state of emotional chaos have been formulated by Carl Rogers, who advocates that the interviewer manifest an attitude of warmth, genuineness and empathy. He has shown how open-ended questions that stimulate dialogue are very helpful and also encourage ventilation. An open-ended question or statement such as "Tell me how you feel" builds rapport and trust, while closed-ended questions such as "Are you upset?" elicit quick replies that end dialogue.

Rogers also advocates the use of paraphrase and reflection for rapport building. Paraphrasing involves a brief summary of what the parents are saying. For example, a parent may say "I can't believe that this has happened. It is too much for me to handle. Why would such a thing happen to our family?" The interviewer responds by stating empathically, "You really are shocked and upset by this," thus paraphrasing what has been said as well as accurately reflecting back the feelings expressed. Literal, empathic interpretation of a client's feelings is referred to as "active listening."

Do not ask parents of sexually abused children in a crisis condition to make evaluations or find causes. Do not ask them "Why did this happen?" Instead, say "Let's talk about how you feel." Be supportive and reassuring. Deal with the current problem. Use the language of the parent. Finally, if necessary, give direction. People in crisis often need someone to be in control, to supply answers and guidance. For example, speak with authority when telling parents not to overreact or blame the child, and advise them that they can cause harm to the child by assuming such attitudes. Let them know that they can and should talk with their youngster about the molestation—but that their role must be strictly supportive. Inform them that all cases of molestation must be reported, and that the child may be required to testify in a court proceeding.

Follow-up in crisis situations is useful and often necessary. Parents should be informed of your ongoing interest. Let them know that you would be willing to telephone the child weekly in order to offer support.

## Interviewing Offenders

In most cases, sexual offenders are interviewed first by the police or Child Protective Services social workers. On occasion, however, physicians, counselors, nurses, and teachers may be the first authority figures to talk with child molesters. In a recent case, an incest offender, guilty of about two years of sexual involvement with his daughter, decided to tell his wife about his offenses. He stayed home from work one day in order to build the courage to confess. By the time his spouse returned from her job late in the afternoon, this man was suffering from severe anxiety and was quite incoherent. He kept repeating the same phrase, ''I have to talk.'' Paramedics, called to intervene, took the offender to a local hospital where he was admitted for an evaluation. That evening he began to talk with his sympathetic nurse about his early childhood and suddenly he disclosed incestuous involvement with his daughter. The nurse was nonjudgemental and empathic. As a result, this offender felt relief immediately. The following morning he confessed to the police, knowing that he would be charged with child molestation.

The very same techniques that are used with victims and their families are effective with offenders. If an offender is judged or confronted, he will resist all attempts to elicit information from him. Since he fears imprisonment and disruption of family life, the typical incest offender will deny his behavior. He, like the pedophile, is confused, frightened, and above all, emotionally disturbed. The pedophile is a potentially valuable informant who not only fears incarceration but also the label of MDSO (mentally disordered sex offender).

Treating the sex offender without condemnation often confuses him and subtly encourages him to ventilate and disclose information that he otherwise would not reveal. An attitude reflecting warmth, genuiness and concern will facilitate dialogue. It is important to note that the skills and approaches used by individuals in the helping professions are not necessarily the same as those used by law enforcement. Police officers usually approach offenders in a confronting manner. It is their role to determine the exact nature of crimes committed and appropriate charges to be filed. On the other hand, the therapist's role is to help; but she or he also is mandated to report suspected or known abuse. On first contact, offenders should be advised that any form of child sexual abuse will be reported to the authorities.

Reporting child sexual abuse is mandated by law. The abuse will not end unless it is reported. Reporting and the ensuing legal process also will assist the victim's recovery because such actions will help to demonstrate to the child that what was done to him or her was wrong and illegal. It will also demonstrate that society views the adult, not the child, to be responsible for the wrong which was done. Legal action is necessary to offset the short- and long-term effects of sexual abuse. These effects are described more completely in the next chapter.

# 4

# Effects of Sexual Abuse

Victims of both incestuous abuse and pedophilia suffer from a wide range of symptoms. Behaviorally, they may experience personal, social, sexual and academic adjustment problems. Physically, they may suffer from chemical addictions and numerous psychosomatic disorders. Psychologically, they often feel depressed, suicidal, self-destructive, ashamed and guilty.

## Incest

In terms of manifest symptoms, the effects of incestuous abuse can be similar to the effects of pedophilia or child rape. There are, however, some fundamental differences which stem from the fact that incest involves a complex array of variables, which are related both to family dynamics and to the fact that incest victims usually are female. These differences are important and determine therapeutic goals, treatment strategies, and prognoses.

## Effects on the Victim

A female victim of incest tends to appear quite precocious. This is because her role in the family has been sexualized and because she has been forced into the role of wife in the family. Many women who were molested as children claim that they were robbed of their childhood and they feel that their early needs for appropriate nurturance were not met. Because their emotional development has been arrested, child victims often demonstrate a pseudomaturity that masks their need for normal parental affection.

Feelings of responsibility for what has happened and resultant guilt over it appear to be somewhat intensified in victims of incest. One reason for intensified guilt relates to the complex intrafamilial dynamics and to the fact that these youngsters already have had relationships with the offenders prior to the onset of incest. They reason that they "could have done something" to prevent incest or to stop the abuse once it started.

Guilt also is compounded by the fact that most victims do not disclose incest when it first starts. When they do tell someone, their guilt is exacerbated because of the ramifications of disclosure. Will Dad go to jail? What about the family income? Will the family dissolve?

Victims feel responsible for incest partly because, unconsciously or consciously, they know it is wrong. They wonder, Why me? Why is Dad seeking sexual fulfillment from me instead of Mom or from another adult female? Some victims wonder why they were chosen instead of one of their siblings. These feelings intensify alienation from family and peers and a sense of being somehow "different."

Victims' loss of trust in authority figures is one of the most devastating effects of incest. Their parents are the first adults children learn to trust, and incest represents the ultimate betrayal of that trust. Hence, victims tend to be suspicious of authority figures and, in therapy, are slow to open up and reveal their true feelings. It is quite common for victims first to tell their peers about the occurrence of incest in the family. Having learned to be wary of adults, they tend to fear confiding in them and may also doubt that an adult will believe what they say.

These issues related to trust, responsibility, intimacy, thwarted needs for nurturance and blocked affect have long-term implications for incest victims, who later experience a variety of problems as they seek mature adult relationships. It is particularly difficult for victims to trust males or to establish deep and intimate interpersonal relationships. In addition, women whose early needs were neglected lack basic skills in parenting their own young.

Because of the complexity of feelings resulting from incestuous abuse, many victims experience a high level of repressed rage. Consequently we see anger turned inward as these victims become involved in a variety of self-destructive behaviors including suicide threats and attempts, self-mutilation, chemical abuse and prostitution. When they marry, some victims set the stage for molestation of their daughters either to relive vicariously their own unresolved trauma, to avoid intimacy with their spouses, or as an expression of displaced anger. Victims not only feel anger toward their fathers but also toward their mothers—and toward themselves for submitting to their fathers and protecting their mothers. (See Table 4-1.)

## Effects on the Family

Effects of incestuous abuse on the offender and spouse have not been dealt with sufficiently in the literature. Because they drastically influence the entire family, these effects are important for professional workers to understand. Some offenders are imprisoned for their actions; others are given short-term jail sentences and probation. Many fathers are convicted of child molestation within the family and then returned to the home within a relatively short period of time.

# Table 4-1: Summary of Common Short- and Long-Term Effects of Child Sexual Abuse

**Short-Term**                                           **Long-Term**

**Physical**
- Urogenital/anal injuries and irritation
- Presence of semen (vaginal, rectal, oral)
- V.D. (oral, rectal, urogenital)
- Anal enlargement
- Pregnancy
- Psychosomatic symptoms

**Behavioral**
- Affective problems (depression, fears/phobias, guilt, anger, low self-esteem, self-blame, alienation, detachment)------------------------->
- Social withdrawal ------------------------------->
- Suicidal tendencies or suicide attempts ------>
- Psychosomatic manifestations------------------>
- Chemical abuse (alcohol and drugs)---------->
- Lack of autonomy------------------------------->
- Lying and manipulation------------------------->
- Sleep disorders (nightmares) ------------------>
- Self-mutilation -------------------------------->
- Sexual promiscuity or aversion to sex ------->
- Seductive behavior ----------------------------->
- Use of precocious sexual language
- Delinquent acting out behavior
- School truancy
- Cruelty to animals
- Functional enuresis/encopresis
- Runaway behavior
- Fear of/aversion to sports
- Regression (thumb-sucking, babytalk)
- Autoerotic preoccupation (excessive masturbation)

- Homophobia
- Homosexuality
- Time-bomb effect/ post traumatic stress reaction
- Problems with parenting
- Sexual dysfunction
- Relationship problems (trust/intimacy)
- Splitting/dissociative and conversion states
- Multiple personality
- Psychosis
- Child molestation

Once the offender is back in the home, he may experience a drastic role change from his customary position as dominant father figure. Mothers become suspicious and watchful. They often express anger and jealousy toward their husbands in very passive-aggressive ways. In some cases, jealousy of the victim is expressed by a wife's attempt to strip her husband of all parental responsibility, degrade his masculinity or subvert his role as family protector.

A mother generally has a complex reaction to incest. She, too, feels guilty and responsible. As a result, she punishes her spouse and sometimes her daughter. Punishing her husband is one way to compensate for having been unaware of the abuse on a conscious level. Self-punishment through chronic depression or anxiety also relieves guilt. Punishment directed toward the victim is a more complicated phenomenon. Basically, a mother unconsciously is saying to herself, "If I punish you, you were wrong and responsible; therefore I no longer have to feel guilty."

Jealousy is another common reaction found in mothers of incest victims. A mother often sees her daughter as a rival for her spouse's attention, and hence, becomes over-attentive to the daughter's clothing, manner of behavior, dating partners, etc,

Also because of guilt, some mothers allow their daughters an unlimited degree of freedom, or actually help to perpetuate irresponsible behaviors. In one family, for example, the mother allowed the former victim of long-term father-daughter incest to return home at age twenty, pregnant, with two out-of-wedlock children. No demands were made upon the daughter to seek therapy, vocational assistance or financial aid. The mother worked at three jobs in order to support this young woman and her children.

It is important to note that generalizations about incestuous families provide us with a stereotypical picture that can be harmful or helpful. Such profiles clearly do not fit all individual families or situations. Applying the "textbook picture" to every case may do irrevocable disservice both to clients and the professionals who seek to assist incestuous families. On the other hand, professionals who are alert to standard warning signs can play an important intervention role in cases of sexual abuse.

The following case study illustrates the importance of professional alertness:

> *Thirteen-year-old Michelle ran away from home for the third time in sixteen months. This time, however, she ran to a youth shelter, where she advised the counselor on duty that she did not like her natural parents because they were too strict.*
>
> *The counselor questioned Michelle at length and learned that she had been a good student until two years before, when her grades began to drop. She admitted to having abused marijuana, amphetamines and alcohol with regularity, and to having been sexually active with two different boys in the past month. Since the age of eleven, Michelle had attempted suicide twice, once by taking twenty aspirin and once by slashing her wrists. She claimed that she did not like either of her parents and had no intention of returning home.*
>
> *Because the counselor was alert to symptoms of sexual abuse, she asked Michelle directly if she had been abused in any way. Michelle claimed that her father "used a belt on me" last year but at first she denied sexual molestation. Upon further questioning, the youngster admitted that she had been sexually abused by her father from age nine until two months ago, when molestation had finally ceased because she had threatened to tell someone.*
>
> *Child Protective Services and the police were notified. Charges were filed against the father,*

> *who at first denied incestuous involvement with Michelle but later admitted to abuse when he learned that he would be required to take a polygraph test and that his daughter might have to testify in court.*
>
> *The girl's mother insisted that her husband was innocent and that Michelle was a "slut." Even after the father admitted his offense, the woman maintained that Michelle had encouraged his advances.*

The picture presented in this case is a fairly typical one. Incest was not disclosed until the victim reached her teen years. She was reluctant to talk about the abuse for fear she would not be believed. Michelle, however, presented symptoms (recent acting-out behaviors including running away, school problems, chemical abuse and sexual relations with peers) that alerted the counselor who questioned her at length. The fact that she had fled to a shelter indicated that Michelle, like so many abused girls, wanted to disclose incestuous involvement in the home.

As in so many cases, the father originally denied allegations; but, like most incestuous fathers, he loved his daughter and did not want her to endure the ordeal of court involvement. (He also feared the results of a polygraph test.)

Probably because of jealousy and guilt, the mother did not assume a protective stance toward her child. Rather than face her and her spouse's own sexual and marital issues, she chose to displace blame and anger onto her daughter.

The counselor's intervention did create a new crisis for Michelle and her family. However, without such intervention, Michelle and her family could not have taken the first step toward recovery.

# Pedophilia

The effects of pedophilic activities on young victims appear to depend on various factors—particularly age of the victim at the time of onset, frequency of the activity, intensity of the activity, and the victim's relationship to the perpetrator. Obviously, a ten-year-old boy approached by a pedophile in a movie theater on a single occasion will suffer less trauma than will a seven-year-old youngster involved in long-term pedophilic activities. In general, the effects of child sexual abuse can be and often are very devastating.

Short-term effects may be openly or more subtly manifested. They may begin with expressions of shock, fear, anxiety, crying and restlessness. There may be eating or sleeping disorders, soreness, discharge or bleeding. Short-term effects also may include feelings of being different and alienated, extreme or acute guilt and anger. These are often manifested by a variety of psychosomatic complaints including headaches, stomachaches, enuresis and a generalized tension syndrome.

Both long- and short-term effects include painful urination, encopresis, enuresis and conversion symptoms such as abdominal pain. Other physical complications include pregnancy, venereal disease and vaginal or rectal infections. Behaviorally, the child who has been sexually abused may become irritable, withdrawn and depressed. She or he may act out in the home or community, become sexually promiscuous or take drugs. Excessive masturbation, autoerotic behavior, sexual curiosity and seductiveness also are characteristic of sexually abused youngsters. In general, the prognosis for a normal sexual adjustment may be guarded.

Long-term effects on victims can be equally devastating. Many of these children become runaways who prostitute themselves for a place to live and food to eat. Later, they may become child molesters, pimps or criminals. Long-term effects also can include continued sleep disorders characterized by dreams and nightmares, phobias and changes in behavior. There may be a fear of school, fear of men, or of being alone. Some of these fears involve displacement, i.e., fear of the offender is displaced onto other persons or situations. Few children experience total absence of symptoms.

## Male Victims of Sexual Abuse

Follow-up studies on sexually abused boys indicate that they tend to internalize the trauma and to react through self-destructive activities resulting in such characteristics as obesity, anorexia, self-mutilation, suicide, self-medication, or depression. Some boys completely externalize the trauma through acts of child abuse, spousal abuse or murder. Girls generally tend to internalize trauma and often react self-destructively.

Other symptoms of victims include hyperactivity, excitability, recurring fears, nightmares and crying spells. Behaviorally, they may act out in the home and community through defiance, delinquent acts and drug or alcohol abuse. These are angry, confused children who blame themselves for the abuse they suffered and who persistently ask "Why me? What is different about me? What is wrong with me?" On some level, almost all of the victims feel responsible for what happened to them.

One common long-term effect, experienced especialy by male victims, relates to psychosexual confusion and an identity crisis. Some boys fear homosexuality or become homosexuals. An example is found in one young man who was sexually molested for a period of six months when he was ten years old:

> The offender was a 28-year-old pedophile the boy had met at a swimming club. As a youngster, the victim never reported the molestation. Later, in counseling, he reported suffering from long-term chronic depression, low self-image and a persistent fear of homosexuality. He claimed that he felt a strong need to prove and assert his manhood. For this reason, as soon as he graduated from high school he married an unattractive, dominant mother figure, the mother of a six-year-old daughter, who was ten years older than he. He probably chose this particular

*marital partner because of his underlying self-doubts and negative self-image; even more probably, because he was emotionally fixated at the age he had been when molested and needed a strong mother just as he had at age ten.*

*During the early years of his marriage, this man was hyper-sexual, requiring sexual intercourse five to six times daily. He performed quickly and in a cursory fashion so that his spouse never was able to experience pleasure during or before intercourse. If she ever acted as the aggressor, or ever assumed a dominant role during the sex act, he became impotent. Unconsciously, he may have associated dominance with maleness. Fears of homosexuality were renewed when his wife assumed control during love making.*

*After two years, the wife became pregnant. She had no desire to have sex during her pregnancy and her husband felt totally rejected. Again, his manhood was in question. It was during this time that he began to molest his eight-year-old stepdaughter. Molestation was an expression of anger and retaliation in the face of spousal rejection. It also served as a vehicle to assert manhood, since a child poses no real threat to a man who questions his potency. Finally, molestation was an infantile reaction to perceived sexual rejection, a reaction similar to that of a ten-year-old boy.*

From this case history we see that, in boys who have been molested by male offenders, fear of homosexuality may be an issue requiring resolution. Fear of homosexuality or of accusations of homosexual behavior are reasons boys often fail to report abuse.

(Some boys who experience pleasure during molestation, who identify with the assailant and participate during the molestation, do become homosexuals later in life.)

Boys also may fail to report abuse because of shame and guilt over pleasurable aspects of the molestation. The shame these youngsters experience is not always related to sexual contact. Some boys are ashamed simply because they have been physically over-powered by an older male.

## Female Victims of Sexual Abuse

Women who have been sexually abused often have problems with trust and intimacy in later life. Some of these victims have multiple marriages, some become lesbians and others suffer from various forms of sexual dysfunction. Female victims may become indiscriminate or promiscuous in their choice of sexual partners, thus confirming their unconscious belief that all relationships are sexual and that they are merely sexual objects to others. Others may become withdrawn sexually and avoid physical intimacy as a reaction to early molestation. In addition, the need to maintain self-control and to control others often occurs as a reaction to the sense of powerlessness experienced as a young child. Maintaining control during sexual relations results in lack of satisfaction and may be a reaction to past ego-alien pleasures experienced during early molestation.

Often female victims (or survivors* as they prefer to be called), seek father figures in the men with whom they have intimate relationships. Unfortunately, in a number of instances, the father figures tend to express their dominance in abusive ways. Thus, alcoholism, wife battering and child sexual abuse bear high correlations to each other. Choosing an abusive partner

---

* Victims often prefer to think of themselves as survivors for a number of reasons. The term "survivor" is a positive one that connotes strength, growth and independence. Many survivors rightly believe that even though they were victimized at one time, they are not life-long victims subject to continued or repeated abuse by others.

unconsciously serves to reinforce low self-esteem in women who were molested as children.

Several psychiatrists and psychologists, Joseph Peters among them,* have referred to the time-bomb effect of child rape. If issues are not resolved, the trauma of child rape becomes renewed later in life. Frequently at times of critical change, such as marriage and childbirth, the victim may become psychotic or disoriented. The time-bomb effect seems particularly severe with women molested at a young age who have successfully repressed the trauma.

One woman, symptom-free for most of her life, began to experience destructive and self-destructive behavior at age 34. Paramedics had to be called to restrain the woman and she was hospitalized on two occasions following particularly severe episodes. Long-term therapy helped her to remember early years of father-daughter incest between her second and fifth years of age. Once early sexual abuse was uncovered, the violent episodes this woman was experiencing could be explained. A seductive relationship between the woman's current husband and her stepdaughter had reactivated forgotten conflicts.

Parenting can be and often is especially difficult for adult women who were molested as children. Because their own needs were thwarted in childhood, often they are unable to nurture their offspring and they feel jealous of adult attention displayed toward their children. Many resort to the use of chemicals to relieve stress and to enable them to cope with the problems of everyday life. A large percentage of alcohol-abusing women were molested as children. Over 70% of female drug addicts and prostitutes have a history of sexual abuse.

Preliminary findings released by research analyst Debra Boyer in 1980 indicate that there also is a correlation between early sexual abuse and male prostitution.Thirty-six percent of male prostitutes

---

* Peters, J. "Child Rape: Defusing a Psychological Time Bomb." *Hospital Physician*, February, 1973.

questioned in Boyer's study (which was funded by a National Institute of Mental Health grant) stated that they were raped one or more times before they reached the age of thirteen. The incidence of acknowledged rape was even greater for the 70% of the sample who identified themselves as homosexual.

Elias (1982) reported on interviews with 200 street prostitutes. Sixty percent were sixteen years old or younger. More than 75% stated that they had been raped, most around the age of ten. More than 40 of those interviewed said they had attempted suicide before they became prostitutes.*

Judianna Densen-Gerber, founder of Odyssey House, a residential drug abuse facility in New York City, has reported that in her 1975 sample of 118 female inpatients, 44% had been victims of incest; 75% had been sexually abused before the age of 12; and 45% had been abused before the age of nine.

Psychological responses to incest range from hysterical reactions to psychosis. Hysterical reactions include conversion reactions (motor paralysis) and dissociative states (wanderings, spells of absence, convulsions and splitting of personality/multiple personality). Psychotic reactions include schizophrenia and depressive psychosis (suicide and self-mutilation).

# Conclusion

In general, the effects of sexual abuse are less damaging if the abuse was short-term and committed by a stranger without the threat or use of coercion. Effects also will be minimized if adults are supportive to the victim and if counseling is made available. Such knowledge should help all professionals who work with children to realize the value of their awareness and support for victims of child sexual abuse. This knowledge also has important implications for the treatment of children who have been sexually abused.

---

* Elias, T. "Young Female Prostitutes." *The Press*, Vol. 10, #5, October 1982, p. 29.

# 5

# Implications for Treatment

Traditionally, authorities have grouped all sexual offenses, making few if any distinctions among the various types of perpetrators (pedophiles, incest offenders and rapists) and their motivations for abuse/assault. In recent years, however, we have begun to make important distinctions, both among offenses and offenders, which are enabling us to formulate more accurate prognoses and treatment strategies.

## Incest

Until fairly recently, incest offenders were treated like other sexual offenders. They were removed from the home and seen in individual therapy following prison terms and/or concomitant with probation. Recently alternative treatment models have been developed which involve the entire family.

## The Giarretto Model

Several years ago, a therapist in California, Dr. Henry Giarretto, devised a treatment model for incest offenders and their families. The program that Giarretto developed is called C.S.A.T.P. (Child Sexual Abuse Treatment Program) and P.U./D.S.U. (Parents United/Daughters and Sons United). Giarretto's model has been so successful that it has spread nationwide, with many chapters operating throughout the country.

The program has been carefully evaluated and has been deemed successful for two primary reasons. First, it is cost-effective to the taxpayer  because it eliminates lengthy prison sentences for offenders and foster care costs for the state. Second, it decreases the recidivism rate. Giarretto maintains that only two to five percent of the offenders in his program remolest in the home. However, a number of experts in the field of child sexual abuse believe the recidivism rate may be much higher.

Child Sexual Abuse Treatment Program and Parents United/ Daughters and Sons United, which is victim-oriented, is based on the premises that victims generally want their families to remain intact and that there is a better prognosis for their future adjustment if they are given the opportunity to work through issues in a family-oriented treatment program. Giarretto believes that many incest offenders can be rehabilitated and that prison will not help these men. Offenders, however, must take full responsibility for their acts, must agree to long-term therapy, and must receive some punishment (short-term jail, for example) in order to be eligible to enter the program. Rapists, pedophiles, and severe antisocial personalities are not considered for acceptance into C.S.A.T.P.— P.U./D.S.U.

The program involves the cooperation and joint efforts of Child Protective Services, adult probation, the police and the court system. Once an offender is arrested, he is evaluated for acceptance into the program. If he is assessed as treatable and if he admits to the charges of child molestation, he is permitted to enter a plea bargain. In exchange for a short-term jail sentence (with possible work furlough), he enters a two-year group therapy program called Parents United. Whether or not they plan to remain with their spouses, wives also become part of the program. Victims are referred to Daughters and Sons United groups for on-going support.

The offender is not allowed back into the home for a period of months following release from jail. He remains in group treatment for two years and is seen for individual (and/or marital) therapy as well. He is provided with a sponsor and may become involved in community work geared toward enlightening others about incestuous abuse.

Group work is both supportive and confronting. It involves offenders, spouses, couples and children's groups. All acts of recidivism are reported and offenders, if they remolest, are immediately referred back to the courts for prison terms.

The program, which has been likened to Alcoholics Anonymous in some respects, appears to be successful despite the fact that many people consider it quite controversial. Support and understanding are offered in a humanistic setting while, at the same time, a firm approach is used to monitor behaviors. In addition, families are afforded an opportunity to work through their conflicts and remain intact.

One important point to remember is that pedophiles and rapists are not considered for acceptance into this program. The dynamics of incest are different from those of other sexual offenses. The incest offender rarely is seen as fixated; ie., he does not have a set compulsion to molest as does the pedophile. In addition, unlike the rapist or pedophile, the incest offender has much to lose if he remolests. He is heavily invested in his family and in reestablishing unity among family members.

A second important point relates to the fact that not every incest offender is accepted into Giarretto's program. Those offenders who molest outside of the family as well as within the family are classified as pedophiles. Perpetrators who persist in denying incestuous involvement, who show no remorse or guilt—and/or who have an unusual or particularly lengthy history of molesting— are ineligible. (See Table 5-1.)

# Table 5-1: Issues to Consider When Predicting Recidivism of Sexual Offenders

1.  Childhood

    *   History of behavioral, social and school problems (fighting, temper tantrums, belligerence, school problems, poor peer relations)

    *   Presence of sociopathic triad of pyromania, enuresis and cruelty to animals (Hellman and Blackman, 1966)

    *   History of poor parenting (child abuse, child sexual abuse, lack of parental supervision, poor father identification, maternal deprivation)

    *   Juvenile record

2.  Adulthood

    *   Impaired or low mental/intellectual functioning

    *   Presence of (violent) fantasies and/or paranoid delusions

    *   History of prior (arrests for) sex crimes

    *   Presence of high stressors in the environment

    *   History of poor adaptive strategies with reference to internal and external stressors (displaced anger, flight reactions)

- Chronic low self-esteem and feelings of powerlessness

- Low tolerance for frustration/impulsiveness

- Depersonalization of others, i.e., absence of guilt, remorse and empathic responses

- Limited capacity for insight

- History of employment/military instability

- Egocentric behavior/orientation to self

- Inability to tolerate criticism or frustration

- Primary defenses of rationalization, denial and projection

- Manipulative, expedient and action-oriented behavior

- Shallow affect characterized by objectifying others

- History of repeated interpersonal conflicts

- Evidence of psychotic/pre-psychotic behavior

Victims treated in the program have the same therapeutic needs as victims of extrafamilial molestation. Their principal needs are to:

1. establish trusting and honest relationships;

2. develop positive self-image and self-concept;

3. overcome internalized guilt and self-blame;

4. learn to communicate feelings and needs verbally;

5.  strengthen impulse control by channelling energies in
    socially acceptable ways;

6.  develop better coping skills and behaviors;

7.  learn alternate means of expressing tensions (symptom
    relief);

8.  work through the trauma associated with the abuse; and

9.  explore (intrafamilial) relationships with the aim of
    resolving feelings about family members involved in the
    molestation.

Giarretto's model is one of the most comprehensive and
best-known nationally. Similar models are based on an approach
where dysfunction is seen from the viewpoint of the family as a
system (family systems approach) rather than as a group of people
with individual pathology. Hence, individual choice and responsibility may tend to be minimized for the offender. Mother is seen
as a silent, collusive partner in incestuous abuse, i.e., as "the
cornerstone in the pathological family system."* Families are seen
as highly disturbed with role confusion, indirect communication
and poorly defined boundaries.**

By contrast, there are a number of other approaches currently
being used with members of incestuous families, both by individual
therapists and by groups of therapists practicing in mental health
centers. For example, among victim advocates, punishment of the
offender is encouraged. Incest is seen as a crime, not an illness

---

* Lustig, N. "A Family Group Survival Pattern," Archives of *General Psychiatry*, # 14,
1966, 31-40.

** Kennedy, M. & Cormier, B. M. "Father-Daughter Incest: Treatment of the Family,"
Papers of the American Society of Criminology. Columbus, OH: Columbus State University,
1965, 143-149.

that is symptomatic of family pathology. The notion of the colluding mother is refuted by a number of authorities who believe that it is counterproductive to hold wives accountable for their husbands' offenses.*

Children are perceived as vulnerable and in need of protection. Validation of their innocence results from incarceration of the offender. To that end, child victims are encouraged to testify against offenders in court. Family therapy is not seen as necessary to help victims work through the trauma of incestuous abuse. Separate treatment for victims and offenders is advocated.**

Currently, there are a number of institutional, community-based and self-help sex offender treatment programs in the United States. Many of these programs have been developed to treat offenders singly rather than in the family context. However, it is not uncommon for wives to be invited to participate in some aspects of therapy.***

Therapeutic modalities can range from behavioral aversive conditioning to chemical castration, but most programs incorporate common approaches including educational and social skills development, stress management, sex re-education and treatment of sexual inadequacies. Usually, there is direct confrontation regarding sexual offenses, control issues, reality versus fantasy in thought and action and depersonalization of victims.****

## Survivors

One of the most valuable approaches to dealing with survivors of incestuous abuse, and the method most generally recommended,

---

* Lucy Berlinger, Sexual Assault Center, Harborview Medical Center, Seattle, as reported in: Stark, E. The Unspeakable Family Secret. *Psychology Today*, May, 1984, p. 42.

** Ledray, L. "Victims of Incest." *American Journal of Nursing*, August, 1984.

*** Female incest offenders and pedophiles do exist but the vast majority do not come to the attention of the authorities. In addition, male perpetrators far outnumber their female counterparts.

**** For additional information, refer to: Brecher, E.M. *Treatment Programs for Sex Offenders*. Washington, D.C.: U.S. Department of Justice, Law Enforcement Assistance Administration, 1978, which surveys twenty sex offender programs throughout the United States.

involves the semistructured group focusing on both experiential and didactic work. Survivors readily identify with one another, and shared empathic responses are immediate, powerful and very therapeutic, particularly in facilitating catharsis.

Preferably, all clients should have completed individual therapy and should be screened prior to entering the group. Screening is relatively simple. It involves precluding admission of women with severe psychopathology (mainly psychotics and multiple personalities). The groups generally are ongoing and designed to provide support and empathic sharing.

Didactic material includes information on assertiveness, sexuality and sexual dysfunction, victimization, communication skills, and chemical abuse and other self-destructive behaviors. Bibliotherapy is a valuable tool used to impart didactic material. The focus is on assigning clients reading materials that are related to sexual abuse and that include first-person accounts. Guest speakers from police departments, rape crisis centers and self-defense schools often are invited to particular group sessions.

Experiential work focuses on blocked affect, particularly guilt and anger. Because incest survivors often have repressed affect associated with early abuse, experiential work is invaluable to the group experience and necessitates a high level of expertise from the therapist. Spontaneous catharsis is facilitated by journal sharing and reading excerpts from first-person accounts. Bioenergetics is effective for anger release, along with a variety of gestalt techniques.

The Unsent Letter to the Offender, used with teenagers and older children, is one example of a powerful technique that rarely fails to elicit blocked affect. The instructions for adults are the same as for child victims. The client is asked to write a letter to the offender expressing her feelings about him, the abuse he perpetrated and the effects of this abuse on her. She then reads this letter to the group, often repeatedly, until verbal expression matches the intensity of the content. Inevitably, strong affective reactions are elicited.

Techniques for group work with survivors vary, depending on the expertise and orientation of facilitators, but the goals remain the same. They are to:

1. validate individual worth;

2. share the commonality of the incest experience and its aftermath;

3. decrease guilt, self-blame and responsibility for the abuse on the part of the victim;

4. impart educational information;

5. teach assertive behaviors via education, role plays and modeling; and

6. release blocked affect, thus facilitating identification and labeling of emotions.

Goals for group work are essentially the same as those for individual sessions and many of the same techniques can be employed. If a client is not ready to enter a group, it is helpful to establish preliminary counseling with two or three survivors meeting together. Judith Herman and Emily Shatzow have developed a time-limited group therapy program for incest survivors. In order to enter a group, survivors must be functioning reasonably well, participating in individual therapy, and lacking ambivalence about involvement in a group with incest survivors. The group is structured with ground rules, goal setting, factual information, support, and the opportunity to ventilate and share experiences.*

---

* Paper presented at the 135th Annual Meeting of the American Psychiatric Association, Toronto, Canada, May 15-21, 1982.

## Working With Adolescents

Group work is the preferred modality for treating incestuously abused teenagers. The model is similar to that used for survivors. Sometimes it is possible to form successful heterogeneous groups composed of selected older adolescents, survivors and mothers. Individuals in heterogeneous groups must not be related or even known to one another. While a heterogeneous mix is possible, even sometimes beneficial, it is not wise to mix delinquent girls with those who are not acting out, due to possible negative effects of the contagion factor.

With adolescents, it is important to limit didactic presentations and to make sure the material is interesting and relevant. Presentations should be informal, lively and of short duration. Important topics to include in lectures and discussions include sexuality, chemical abuse and suicidal behavior.

To break through defensive barriers and to help the youngsters release blocked affect, group work with teenagers often involves confrontation. A fair amount of expertise is required when working with this population, since many teenage victims are emotionally fragile, with low impulse control. Masked affect can be mistaken for stability. Thus, confrontation should be used sensitively and only when a high degree of trust has been established. Confrontation must be tempered with caring and support.

In the last few years authorities have been identifying a larger and larger population of molested teenage boys, many of whom were themselves molesting younger children. Molested adolescent males may comprise as much as twenty-five to thirty percent of the caseloads of professionals. The sexual abuse of boys is underreported for many reasons including humiliation, shame, and fear of the stigma associated with victimization by males.* These victims displace their anger by sexually assaulting younger

---

* Nielson, T. "Sexual Abuse of Boys: Current Perspectives," *The Personnel and Guidance Journal*, November, 1983.

children. They need experiential therapeutic interventions to release their feelings, as well as behavioral controls to monitor their actions and alter dysfunctional responses to stress.

Group therapy with male adolescent sex offenders necessitates use of male and female co-therapists for balance and appropriate modeling. Groups are structured, covering both didactic and experiential material:

1. Sex education including factual material, sex-role stereotyping, and issues related to gender identity

2. Social skills training including communication and assertiveness

3. Stress management including impulse control and behavioral change

4. Clarification of values and goals

5. Decision-making and conflict resolution

6. Victim issues including victimization (displaced anger and identification with the aggressor), the effects of victimization, and depersonalization

7. Early life trauma such as child physical and sexual abuse

8. Self-destruction including chemical abuse, suicide and self-mutilation

9. Affective issues including anger, fear, guilt, shame, and empathy

Therapeutic modalities and techniques are varied and include role plays, bibliotherapy, use of video/audio resources, marathons, guided imagery, initiative games, behavioral contracting and expressive arts. Restitution through community volunteer work improves self-image and a sense of commitment to an altered lifestyle. Finally, reenactments of victimization and victim-confrontation sessions have proved effective in eliciting appropriate empathic responses in young offenders.

**Working With Children**

Therapeutic work with children will vary, depending on a number of factors including age of the child, level of mental functioning, degree and frequency of abuse, age at onset of abuse and manifest symptoms. (See Table 5-2.) Another variable is that some children respond readily to therapeutic interventions while others are quite resistant.

With children under the age of five, the therapist focuses on working with the victim's mother, helping her to improve the bonding relationship with her youngster, to develop better parenting skills and to accept concrete guidance in symptom-alleviation. Parents of abused children usually experience severe anxiety about anticipated effects of abuse on their offspring. Often they overreact by projecting their own needs onto those of the child. Supportive sessions, geared toward allowing these parents to ventilate their fears and structured to help them gain insights into their tendencies to project, are effective.

Disclosure of child sexual abuse in the family usually triggers strong emotional reactions from mothers who were molested as children and who have not resolved their own conflicts. These women require individual or group therapy that focuses on their needs as well as those of their offspring.

If a young child is symptom-free, she or he may not need long-term therapy. Nevertheless the parents should be advised to be alert to possible problems that may arise. Parents should learn simple communication skills, such as Active Listening, "I

Messages,'' and attending behaviors, which will encourage the child to ventilate. In addition, parents should know behavioral management techniques that will decrease symptoms in an atmosphere devoid of stress and anxiety.

Occasionally therapists are asked to determine whether or not a young child has been sexually abused. The parent may be concerned because of symptoms the child is exhibiting or because the child has had contact with a suspected molester. Sometimes it is very difficult to make an accurate determination of abuse; consequently, a therapist should never frighten such a child with a barrage of direct questions. Any questions should be worded carefully and based on an overall assessment of the child's level of functioning. The use of play therapy, art therapy and anatomically correct dolls often elicits needed information.

Since they are effective vehicles for working through repressed conflicts in a permissive setting, play and art therapy have many uses with young children. Directed, nondirected, and interactional art therapy also are helpful both in building rapport between the therapist and child, as well as in adjunctive work geared toward helping the youngster express feelings that later can be labeled and processed. A series of techniques and exercises appropriate for use with children can be found in *Incest: A Treatment Manual For Therapy With Victims, Spouses And Offenders* by Mayer, A., Learning Publications, Inc., Holmes Beach, Florida, 1983.

Group work with children under age ten is recommended, provided all youngsters are screened carefully and are thoroughly prepared for the group. Children ages eight to ten feel validated when they can share their experiences with others who also have been molested.

One facet of group work with children sometimes involves preparing the youngsters for the court experience. (See Table 5-3.) The therapist can be a valuable advocate for the child by providing rehearsals of the court process, by serving as a liaison with attorneys, and by being available to answer questions and address concerns. Many cities and counties nationwide now have Victim Witness Programs offering information and assistance in court cases. Victim Witness workers are available to provide transportation to court, accompany the child and/or his/her family to hearings, and educate all concerned regarding any aspect of the court process.

# Table 5-2: Treatment Goals for Incestuously Abused Children

**Without Family Involvement**

1. To stabilize the environmental situation via a protective placement

2. To provide a trustworthy, nurturing and consistent role model via the therapeutic relationship

3. To diminish guilt/blame/sense of responsibility via role-plays and bibliotherapy

4. To help the victim understand inappropriate family dynamics (role reversal, betrayal of trust) via supportive information sharing (Focus is on preventing cycle of negative parenting and teaching victim to nurture self and others)

5. To enhance self-esteem via the therapeutic relationship, assertiveness training and environmental manipulation

6. To teach assertiveness/self-respect

7. To help rechannel acting out and self-destructive behaviors via enhancing self-esteem, and teaching self-control and social skills

8.  To promote catharsis/ventilation of repressed affect (anger, fear) followed by correct labeling of affective states

9.  To diminish compulsive sexual behaviors and the tendency to sexualize all relationships, and to promote a healthy sexual orientation via behavioral change and sex education

10. To alleviate fear/anxiety/alienation via support, nurturing, empathy and understanding

## With Family Involvement

To the above goals, add the following:

1.  Dyad sessions with offender to enhance communication and provide offender with opportunity to accept/ acknowledge feelings of victim and assume full responsibility for molestation

2.  Dyad sessions with the mother to enhance bonding, allow for victim to ventilate and provide the mother with opportunity to assume full responsibility for not protecting victim and for not knowing about molestation

3.  Triad (and/or total family) sessions to solidify gains in dyad sessions, improve communication skills and formulate family goals/plans

# Table 5-3: Glossary of Court Terms for Children and Teenagers

Accuse: to charge a person with breaking the law

Bailiff: the court officer who maintains order in the courtroom

Court Clerk: the court officer who gives witnesses the oath, i.e., promise to tell the truth

Court Reporter: the person who records every word said during the hearing or trial

Defendant: the person accused of breaking the law

Defense lawyer: the lawyer who tries to prove that the defendant is not guilty of the charges against him

Judge: the public official who hears and decides cases in court

Jury: twelve citizens who hear and review the facts before deciding if the defendant broke the law

Lawyer/Attorney: the person who advises clients about legal matters and who represents them in court

Plaintiff: the person who accuses the defendant of breaking the law

Prosecuting Attorney: the lawyer who tries to prove that the defendant is guilty of the charges against him

Victim Witness Program: the group that provides counselors to help victims understand the court proceedings. Victim Witness counselors operate out of the County Attorney's office

In general, the therapeutic community has focused attention on the treatment of female victims of sexual abuse. Recently, more attention is being given to the needs of boys of all ages who have been, or are, victims. Boys comprise a large proportion of molested children.

While it is not methodologically sound to imply causation from correlations, it is equally irresponsible to ignore the clear linkage between a history of child sexual abuse and subsequent patterns of abuse in adult life. Knopp's study of nine programs for treating adolescent sex offenders indicates that high numbers of juvenile sex offenders were molested as children.*

## Working With Mothers

Mothers of victims of incest can be seen individually or in group therapy. For mothers who were molested as children group work often is the appropriate therapeutic modality. Experiences are quickly validated in the group setting and catharsis often occurs spontaneously.

Mothers in the incest triad, like offenders and child victims, should not be stereotyped into categories. Not all mothers can be called Silent Partners; not all have been victims of incest. Many were unaware of the occurrence of abuse in the home; many are not passive and dependent and did not unconsciously enter into collusion with their spouses in the perpetuation of child sexual abuse in the home. Nonetheless, mothers of incest victims share similar concerns that need to be addressed in the therapeutic setting.

---

* Knopp, F.M. *Remedial Intervention in Adolescent Sex Offenses: Nine Program Descriptions.* Syracuse, NY: Safer Society Press, 1982. Five of the programs treating adolescent sex offenders molested as children are: Juvenile Sex Offender Program, University of Washington School of Medicine Adolescent Unit; Program for Healthy Adolescent Experiences, East Community Family Center, Maplewood, Minnesota; Male Adolescent Sex Offender Group, Richfield, Minnesota; The Sexuality Therapy Group, Hennepin County Home School, Minnetonka, Minnesota; and The Sex Offender Therapy Program, Snoqualmie, Washington.

Whether or not they were aware of the abuse, mothers usually feel guilty when they are confronted by the existence of incest in their families. In addition, they tend to harbor anger at themselves, their children and the offender. Self-directed anger stems from guilt which may be more severe in cases where long-term abuse has occurred in the home over a period of years. Anger toward the child is experienced most frequently when disclosure results in additional pain and disruption within the family. Some mothers are angry because their children did not disclose incest to them or to other authority figures sooner. Anger directed toward the offender is understandable—especially in the context of betrayal of family trust.

Because of the guilt, anger and confusion that mothers experience, confrontation is not an advisable tool to use in therapy. A Rogerian approach involving warmth, genuineness and empathy is more effective in building trust and facilitating change. Mothers need to have an opportunity to ventilate their feelings in an accepting setting. If issues related to anger and guilt are not resolved, there is danger of a recurrence of abuse in the home. A mother who is not aware of her feelings of anger or jealousy toward her child may unconsciously establish relationships that expose the youngster to further abuse.

Most mothers in therapy suffer from low self-esteem and many have unmet dependency needs leading to passivity and denial. These women require self-image building, assertiveness training and often a variety of referrals for vocational, educational and financial guidance.

## Working With Offenders

Incest offenders, like mothers and victims, may be seen individually or in group therapy. Some offenders and their wives seek marital and family counseling as well.

Offenders enter therapy for a variety of reasons. Some are mandated to attend sessions prior to or following court hearings;

some seek therapy during incarceration as part of work furlough programs where they are free to work and attend sessions during the day but return to jail at night; and some men, motivated by some renewed personal or family crisis, enter therapy years after incestuous abuse has occurred.

Most therapy programs for men are not geared toward working with all types of sexual offenders. Consequently, it is advisable to establish criteria for admission before accepting any offender for treatment. Generally, men evaluated as appropriate for this type of therapy include those who:

1.  fully admit and take responsibility for the incestuous behavior;

2.  have no prior history of arrests for sexually deviant behavior;

3.  have no history of physical violence;

4.  are not pedophiles or rapists; and

5.  do not suffer from severe diagnosed psychopathology.

Before acceptance for therapy, offenders should commit themselves not to re-molest; to refrain from chemical abuse; to attend appropriate self-help groups such as AA; and to regularly attend all required therapy sessions. Assessment procedures should include a structured interview and a complete socio-sexual history. Copies of prior hospital records or records from mental health professionals should be obtained for the files. Probation and parole officers, along with Child Protective Service workers, should be contacted to establish effective interagency cooperation.

Therapeutic interventions with offenders vary according to individual needs of clients, and a variety of treatment modalities and techniques can be used. Sessions designed to improve self-image are needed, along with referrals to agencies and activities that will increase the offender's support system and emotional and behavioral repertoire. Vocational training and financial aid often are required. Didactic material regarding sexuality and assertiveness usually is included in any therapy program designed to meet the needs of the offenders. Marital or relationship counseling, or family therapy may be indicated. If the offender and his spouse want to keep the family intact, they will need to have dyad and triad sessions with their child. During these sessions, which follow the completion of individual therapy for all three members of the triad, the offender is given an opportunity to apologize to his child for his incestuous behavior, thus alleviating her feelings of guilt and responsibility.

As has been stated previously, a number of incest offenders were themselves molested as children. For these men, experiential probing is necessary because, like women molested as children, they have blocked affect associated with their own molestation. Either they have become molesters through identifying with those who violated them, or they have displaced anger for the person who molested them onto their own victims. In the second instance power over helpless children becomes a vehicle to express blocked feelings of anger and helplessness. Gestalt therapy helps these men to re-experience their own molestation and the feelings associated with their personal trauma. Thus, the offender is helped to recall how it *feels* to be molested, and to gain empathy for his victims.

Behavioral management and environmental manipulation also are important tools when working with offenders. Many offenders continue to fantasize about their victims, and the therapist must help them to distinguish between the thought and the deed. It is important for the offender to gain positive control over his behavior. Simple techniques for avoiding provocative and stimulating situations with children can be of great value. One offender, for example, fantasized about his daughter when she showered before bed. As a tension release, this man began to jog during evening hours when his daughter was preparing for bed.

Work with offenders is difficult because it involves both therapeutic interventions and careful monitoring. Any act of remolestation must be reported. The therapist is placed in a difficult and often tense situation and should make all efforts to build a suitable support network for herself/himself. Such a support system might involve regular clinical staff meetings with co-workers.

# Pedophilia

Due to the distinctive nature of pedophilic activity, the implications for treatment are very different from those for incest. Treatment strategies and success rates for both the offender and the victim will be discussed.

### For The Offender

There is no known treatment for the fixed pedophile although various techniques and modalities are being attempted experimentally. One pedophile summed up the problem when he stated that he was not interested in receiving therapy because, "Once you've tried it (child molestation), it's like tasting ice cream. You want more and more, again and again. . ."

Psychotherapy or traditional "talk therapy" has not generally been effective either with pedophiles, who are fixated, or with rapists, who often have a limited capacity for insight. Psychotherapy alone has little effect in altering fixed patterns of behavior.

In recent years there has been some experimentation with various forms of chemotherapy to treat sexual offenders. Anti-androgen hormones (Depo Provera and Cyproterone) are experimental, and client consent is required for their use. Studies on their effectiveness are limited and inconclusive.

According to Langevin, antiandrogens appear to be both dangerous and ineffective for long-term use because:

1.  They must be used indefinitely.

2.  They affect arousal but not the direction of sexual impulses.

3.  They have serious side effects including infertility, liver damage, diabetes, hot/cold flashes, weight/hair loss (Depo Provera) and testicular atrophy (Cyproterone).

4.  They diminish arousal but not penile reactions.

Another drawback is that while the drugs are in use, they preclude therapeutic interventions. It is not possible to use both drugs and aversive therapy simultaneously for the same end, i.e., to lower arousal.*

Use of Depo Provera and Cyproterone is based on the assumption that hormones cause molestation. To the contrary, research indicates that many men with high testosterone levels do not rape and molest. Finally, chemotherapy may be an ineffective treatment for pedophiles seeking emotional gratification and intimacy from victims rather than pure physical satisfaction.

Incapacitation by voluntary castration has been attempted to prevent recidivism among rapists and other sexual offenders. Here again consent is required, and emotional interest and arousal are not effectively diminished. It is important to note that excision of the testicles does not alter the capacity to attain an erection.

Among the more promising experiments currently being researched are those involving various forms of behavior modification. Behavior modification is based on the principles of learning

---

* Langevin, R. *Sexual Stands: Understanding and Treating Sexual Anomolies in Men.* Hillsdale, New York: Lawrence Erlbaum Associates, Publisher, 1983, p. 58.

theory. The most important assumption behind the theory of modifying behavior is that all behavior is learned and therefore can be unlearned. A second assumption is that two opposite responses cannot exist simultaneously. For example, a person cannot be relaxed and tense at the same time. Thus, successful treatment for the problem of claustrophobia (fear of enclosed spaces) is to teach the client to relax and then gradually expose him or her to closed spaces until the fear is extinguished. With some pedophiles who become anxious and fearful in the presence of adult women, systematic desensitization is used. Here the pedophile gradually is relaxed via deep muscle or autogenic techniques while stimuli are introduced to encourage development of socially acceptable behavior, i.e., erotic responsiveness toward adult females.

Aversion therapy has been tried with a device called a Peter Meter, an elastic apparatus which is wrapped around the penis. Erectile responses are measured while the offender looks at a series of film clips or pictures showing nude female adults or children. In attempting to discourage arousal stimulated by nude children, an aversive odor or a slight electric shock is administered. The goal is to stimulate or encourage appropriate penile responses to adult females.

One problem is that many offenders fantasize about young children while viewing films or photographs of adult women. Secondly, punishment almost never teaches a pedophile to curb his impulses. It is assumed that theoretically the pedophile will, upon release from jail or prison, be motivated to shock himself or self-administer an aversive stimulus if he is aroused by a child. In actual practice, the short-term pleasure the offender experiences at the sight of a child far outweighs any long-term consequences such as a fear of imprisonment. Thirdly, the pedophile may become aversive to the particular sexual object used in therapy, but will respond erotically to other inappropriate stimuli, i.e., other children.

An endless number of other behavioral techniques have been attempted, including hypnotherapy, where a post-hypnotic suggestion is used to inhibit pedophilic behavior. Or the pedophile may be asked to masturbate to a pedophilic fantasy. Just as he reaches climax, he is instructed to alter his image to a socially acceptable one (adult female). Another technique, again drawn from aversion therapy, involves following a pedophilic fantasy with an aversive one (such as being murdered).

Unfortunately, none of these behavioral conditioning techniques has yet proved effective. Professionals simply do not know of a viable modality for the treatment of fixed, compulsive sexual offenders. The sexual offenders program at Atascadero State Hospital in California, once considered quite promising, experienced a serious credibility problem in the early 1980's partly because of public outcry following the release of an offender who subsequently mutilated, molested and killed a young child.

## For The Victim

Therapy for victims of child sexual abuse by pedophiles is much more encouraging than it is for perpetrators. Often, however, the process is quite time-consuming. The length of time depends partly on the prognosis—which, in turn, is related to age of the child, frequency of abuse, duration and intensity of abuse, the support system available to the child and a number of other factors.

Therapy for very young children will differ considerably from that needed by the older child or adolescent. Young children are pre-verbal and unable to label either events or affective states. For this reason, play and art therapy are the recommended treatment modalities. Expressive therapies enable the blocked child to work through trauma or conflict without the necessity of verbalizing or labeling painful emotions or events. The use of anatomically correct dolls has become common practice among therapists who work with small children. The dolls stimulate the child to re-enact traumatic events in a permissive, caring setting where their feelings can be validated.

Older children and adolescents respond well to individual and group work where the focus is on ventilation, release of anger, alleviation of guilt and assertiveness training. Also, for self-image building and for goals or values clarification, a variety of supportive interventions are required.

Ventilation and release of anger are most quickly achieved in a group setting where confrontation can be tempered with support. One useful and commonly-used technique is the Unsent Letter to the Offender. The victim is asked to write a letter to the person who molested her/him, saying how she feels and using any language that expresses her/his feelings. The victim knows that the letter will not be sent; thus she/he feels free to express previously blocked emotions and intense anger. Once the letter has been completed, it is read to the group. These children often break down in tears before they have finished reading the first sentence or two. They always express intense anger and strong feelings of having been deeply wronged.

Guilt and feelings of responsibility for the molestation also are best relieved in a group setting, where the victim senses a commonality of experience with others and where feelings can be validated most effectively. A victim entering group for the first time soon feels relieved. Self-doubts and emotions related to being different from everyone else seem to dissipate as he or she listens to the shared experiences of group members.

Assertiveness training can be accomplished in individual or group settings. Victims need to learn to take care of themselves and to say "no" when their privacy is violated. These children have learned to be victims and they now must unlearn the process.

Clients are first taught to distinguish among three types of verbal and nonverbal behavior—passive, assertive, and aggressive. Once the client understands the three different modes of acting/

reacting, she or he practices assertiveness through role plays in sessions and through reality testing in the outside environment.*

Adult victims require therapeutic interventions similar to those recommended for the older child. They may, however, require specialized work related to sexual dysfunction, problems with intimacy, and stress management.

There are a number of fine books on female sexuality that are of value to therapists and clients alike, including the following:

> Barbach, L. *For Yourself.* New York: Doubleday, 1975.

> Comfort, A. *The Joy of Sex.* New York: Simon and Schuster, 1972.

> Heiman, J. et al. *Becoming Orgasmic: A Sexual Growth Program for Women.* Englewood Cliffs, NJ: Prentice-Hall, 1976.

An adult survivors' group as well as a couples/relationship group are ideal settings in which to focus on issues related to sexuality, interpersonal relationship skills and structured communication exercises designed to enhance intimacy and trust.

In the last few years, we have seen the growth of more effective treatment approaches to sexually victimized children and adults and their families. When motivation is strong, as is often the case with this identified population, therapy can be a gratifying experience for both client and therapist alike.

---

* For complete guidelines on assertiveness training, refer to: Mayer, A. *Incest: A Treatment Manual for Therapy with Victims, Spouses and Offenders.* Holmes Beach, Florida: Learning Publications, 1983.

# 6

# Case Management

*When I was seven, there was this man who came to our school classroom and he said that if we ever had a problem we should go to him. So I went to him with this problem and I was crying and he took me to the principal. The next day this white car came to our house and my dad was mowing the lawn and these two men got out and said that they were taking me away. My dad called them the "f" word and they showed him a paper from the judge and then my dad said to take me. Joey and Sally were crying and I said that I didn't want to go and I was crying too. They wouldn't let me take my clothes or anything. You know what? About a year later I went home and Dad started to molest me again and I just couldn't believe it. Why do you think they took me away instead of him? So this time, I told my friend and she told her mom and her mom told my mom and my mom told me I was lying. She said it didn't*

*happen, that Dad wouldn't do that. Then Dad
slapped my face and he hurt me and I told my
teacher. The social worker came to the school and
I was really scared and she took me to the hospital.
We had to wait forever at the hospital and I kept
telling the social worker that I was hungry. That's
what I said. I was hungry—very very hungry. She
said that I had to be patient. So it must have been
two hours or maybe four hours and then the doctor
saw me and he stuck this thing up me and it hurt
because he was very very very rough. I screamed
alot and the nurse said to squeeze her hand so I
did. And I squeezed it so hard that she told me
to let go so I did. Then the social worker came
in and she told me I could eat in the foster home
and I said that I wasn't going to a foster home.
She said I had to go and when we got there I sat
down and saw all this food on the table and I just
kept looking at it. The social worker said that she
had to get right back to the hospital for another
problem and she'd call later. My foster mom
looked at me in a funny way and I looked at her
and she said, "The social worker didn't even tell
me your name."*

Unfortunately, the above events as reported by an eleven-year
old youngster following long-term sexual abuse by her father are
of a kind that occur all too frequently. Children are damaged by
the system—a system comprised by a network of agencies
employing professionals who are generally overworked, sometimes
"burned out" and often inadequately trained for the tasks at hand.
As a nation we profess to care about our youngsters, but thus far
we have been unable to muster the resources and commitments
needed to validate our concerns and to protect powerless youngsters

from both abusive home situations and the abuses inherent in our system. What is needed is knowledge, coordination and cooperation among all professionals committed to helping to alleviate the trauma of child abuse.

## The Coordinated Team Approach

There are three equally important aspects to the management of child sexual abuse cases. They are the physical/medical, the legal, and the psychological. All three aspects are of vital significance and are closely linked to one another. The physical/medical aspect involves physicians, nurses and pediatric social workers. The legal aspect involves law enforcement and the courts. The psychological aspect involves therapists, social workers, counselors, school counselors and teachers. If a child or the child's parents are interviewed by untrained workers who are not attuned to the family's emotional state and needs, neither victim nor parents will cooperate, and information needed to file charges or to complete a thorough physical examination will be lost. On the other hand, the family that is approached with sensitivity and patience will be more likely to report full and accurate data to legal authorities, to assist in providing a complete medical history, and to cooperate in treating the child for physical complaints and symptoms. In addition, a family whose feelings are considered by case workers will be more amenable to enlisting the services of professional counselors who have been trained for long-term follow-up.

The most effective treatment approach involves a cooperative multi-disciplinary effort. Doctors and nurses are members of a coordinated child abuse team, assessing the presence and extent of physical and emotional trauma, then referring abused patients to legal authorities and therapists for treatment. Following referral, medical personnel remain involved for consultation, information sharing, support and planning. (See Table 6-1.)

## Table 6-1: Typical Agencies and Institutions Involved in Networking Following Disclosure of Child Sexual Abuse

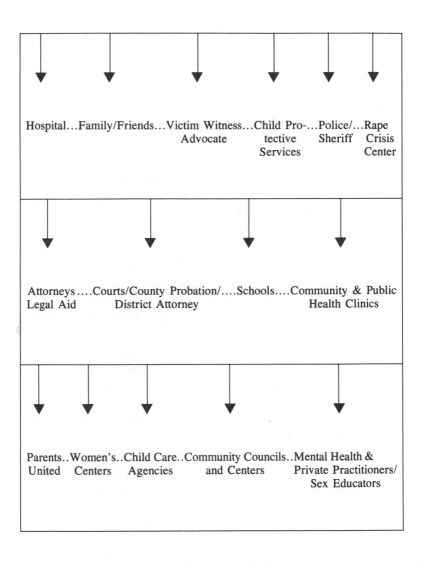

Hospital...Family/Friends...Victim Witness...Child Pro-...Police/...Rape
                                  Advocate          tective    Sheriff   Crisis
                                                    Services            Center

Attorneys....Courts/County Probation/....Schools....Community & Public
Legal Aid        District Attorney                      Health Clinics

Parents..Women's..Child Care..Community Councils..Mental Health &
United   Centers  Agencies        and Centers      Private Practitioners/
                                                        Sex Educators

# Medical Management

Medically, health care professionals have an important role in identifying and managing child sexual abuse. Nurses see child sexual abuse directly (as a result of a presenting complaint) or indirectly (when the child is seen or admitted initially for an unrelated problem). Nurses should be objective in their attitudes toward treatment of victims, evaluating and assessing on the basis of physical and behavioral signs.

Assessment is based on information-gathering (medical, developmental and social history) as well as specimens from laboratory analysis and results of the physical examination. It is important to realize that when there is a suspicion of sexual abuse in the absence of disclosure by the child or family, medical findings serve as corroborative data.

Frequently, there are no obvious physical signs of child sexual abuse. However, evidence may nonetheless be present. Professionals should be alert to the following symptoms:

- Torn or stained underwear

- Physical injury of the external genitalia, vagina, anus, mouth or throat

- Pain on urination

- Poor sphincter control

- Vaginal, rectal or penile discharge, swelling or bleeding of unexplained origin

- Inflammation or infection within the genital area

- Positive acid phosphatase or sperm in female children

- Pregnancy in children under the age of twelve (With pubertal teenage females with evidence of vaginal penetration, advice should be given regarding post-coital prevention of pregnancy)

- Venereal disease or a history of gonorrhea or syphilis in children under the age of twelve

The above symptoms may be indicators of sexual abuse, although some single indicators are not sufficiently conclusive to corroborate molestation. Behavioral indicators include those outlined earlier and are summarized as follows:

- Fears (of the dark, of being alone, of strangers and of new situations)

- Regressive behavior (enuresis, encopresis, thumb-sucking), especially of sudden or unexplained origin

- Personality and behavioral changes (depression, anger, withdrawal, school difficulties, secretiveness)

- Chemical abuse, especially in young children

- Truancy, runaway behavior

- Seductive behavior, public masturbation, excessive masturbation and a preoccupation with sex

Medical personnel should be aware that adolescent victims of brutal sexual assault or rape differ from adult victims in that many of their fears and concerns are directly related to the developmental phase of adolescence. Thus, the trauma of sexual abuse appears to exacerbate issues related to self-image, body image, peer approval and autonomy.

Adolescents are dependent upon their parents. When parents are neither supportive nor understanding an adolescent's recovery from a crisis event is delayed. Some studies have indicated that parents initially react more adversely to sexual assault on their teenagers than do the victims. Normally, parents react openly, with anger focused both on the occurrence of abuse and on the perpetrator.

Burgess, et al.* note that in the aftermath of rape or sexual assault, both parents and teenage victims experience a phase of acute disorganization, which is followed by a phase of long-term reorganization. Parents need to ask questions and receive support and feedback immediately following the assault. The teenage victim, on the other hand, may experience denial, fears, psychosomatic complaints and depression. Schultz** notes that victims sometimes act out in self-destructive ways and that hospital personnel need to be aware of acute emotional reactions, setting limits accordingly.

If the victim is deeply entrenched in denial, she or he may appear not to need psychological interventions. Months later, however, a victim may return for medical care with a variety of psychosomatic complaints. It is the responsibility of hospital personnel to be aware of the link between the original assault and subsequent symptoms that victims may manifest.

Nurses and physicians can best meet the needs of teenage victims by becoming familiar with typical reactions they and their families experience following sexual assault. Problems associated with physical trauma must be addressed first. Then teens should be monitored, provided with support and given needed reassurance. Fears should be addressed openly and directly. Ventilation of emotions should be encouraged. Parents also should be given an

---

* Burgess, A.W., et al., *Sexual Assault of Children and Adolescents*. Lexington, MA: Lexington Books, D.C. Heath & Co., 1978.

** Schultz, L.G., (Ed.), *The Sexual Victimology of Youth*. Springfield, IL: Charles C. Thomas, Publisher, 1980.

opportunity to ventilate and should be encouraged to provide emotional support for their victimized children. (See Table 6-2.)

Items in the following questionnaire are a necessary part of the sexual abuse/assault examination and should be included in the complete medical records of the patient.

1. **Pregnancy History**

   Gravidity _____ Parity _____

   Pregnant _____

   Symptoms of pregnancy _____

2. **Menstrual History**

   Age of menarche _____

   Date of last menses _____

   Last menses normal _____

   Regular menses _____

3. **Sexual Activity**

   Virgin _____

   Most recent coitus _____

   Vaginal tampons used _____

4. **Contraception**

   Past contraception used _____

   Current mode of contraception _____

5. **Venereal Disease**

   Yes _____

   No _____

   Treatments _____

6. **Illnesses**

   Vaginal Infections _____

   Vaginal surgical procedures _____

   Urinary tract infections _____

   Medications _____

7. **Emotional Illnesses**

   Yes _____

   No _____

   Describe _____

8. **Injuries**

   Genital-rectal _____

   Scratches _____

   Lacerations _____

   Intact hyman _____

   Treatments _____

   X-ray _____

   Photographs _____

9.  **Evidence Collected**

    Saline wet mount for sperm

    Present _____          No _____

    Motile _____          No _____

    Urine for pregnosticon

    Yes _____          No _____

    Wet and dry preps from mouth

    Yes _____          No _____

    Urinalysis if bladder trauma

    Yes _____          No _____

    Cervical culture for N. Gonorrhea

    Yes _____          No _____

    Serology

    Yes _____          No _____

    Blood test for syphilis

    Yes _____          No _____

## Table 6-2: Medical Checklist for Sexual Abuse Patients

_____ Attend to immediate needs, i.e., genital, rectal and oral trauma; other physical injuries; symptoms of emotional trauma.

_____ Overall medical history.

_____ Get signatures on release forms.

_____ Conduct physical examination (including, in small children, examination of hymenal ring and vaginal opening).

_____ Collect evidence, take photographs when relevant.

_____ Provide information to parents or guardians on legalities/options.

_____ Notify relevant law enforcement (police) and professional personnel (Sexual Assault Crisis Center)

_____ Supervise medical treatment including tests for presence of sperm (vaginal smear) and tests for V.D.—i.e., blood test for syphilis and cultures for gonorrhea (throat, urethra and vagina). Preventive treatment (penicillin) or recultures for gonorrhea (3-4 weeks) and retests for syphilis (3 months).

_____ Prescribe douches and mouthwash when necessary.

_____ Maintain full records throughout.

_____ Throughout treatment, provide opportunities for patient and family to ventilate emotions; offer your support.

_____ Respond to patient/family questions, or refer to a knowledgeable resource, throughout treatment.

_____ Reassure victim on three critical issues: (1) that reporting assault was correct; (2) that he/she is not alone, and (3) that he/she should not feel guilty (is not responsible).

_____ Make provisions for follow-up medical care in cases of (suspected) venereal disease and pregnancy.

_____ Make provisions for follow-up emotional support through referral and telephone contact.

In addition to the medical information, the police will require complete data on the type and frequency of sexual abuse that has occurred. Since they may be instrumental in providing data to complete the police report, medical personnel should be aware of the information needed by the police. The following questions should be answered for the police:

1. Name of offender, sex, age, date of birth?

2. Whereabouts of offender?

3. Relationship of offender to victim?

4. Age of victim when molestation occurred—dates, times, places?

5. Mother aware of molestation? If so, for how long?

6. Known history of sexual offenses by perpetrator?

7. Types of molestation? For each act, note total number of incidents, duration, prior medical examinations and whether the act was committed by the offender on the victim or by the victim on the offender. Types of offenses are listed below.

    A. Propositioning for sexual acts

    B. Shown pornograhic material

    C. Voyeurism

    D. Exhibitionism

    E. Forced to view sexual acts of others

    F. Fondling (overt kissing, hand/genital contact or manipulation)

    G. Fellatio

    H. Cunnilingus

    I. Simulated intercourse

    J. Attempted penetration (vaginal, anal)

    K. Sodomy (anal intercourse)

    L. Intercourse

    M. Other

RNs and LPNs have more contact with hospitalized patients than other personnel. The sensitivity and concern that nurses demonstrate in helping sexually abused patients often facilitates their recovery from trauma. Guidelines such as those listed below will help nurses deal with patients, their families, and visitors.

## DO

1. *Do* be supportive; listen to feelings; indicate that you care; provide opportunities to talk.

2. *Do* be empathic but neutral.

3. *Do* answer questions honestly when referring family to counselor/law enforcement/attorney for specific answers related to nonmedical aspects of abuse.

4. *Do* monitor the emotional state of the patient. Be aware of "normal" reactions to crisis (fear, shock, numbness, anger).

5. *Do* allow the child to talk in his or her own words.

6. *Do* keep written records regarding disclosures and/or behaviors that may be relevant in court.

7. *Do* make certain that disclosures about sexual abuse are reported—*but* be careful to maintain confidentiality on issues not related to abuse.

8. *Do* be aware of specific hospital policies and procedures on reporting and dealing with child sexual abuse.

9. *Do* make sure family is aware of sexual abuse services. Provide names, addresses and phone numbers of crisis centers.

10. *Do* know your local resources.

11. *Do* serve as a referral resource for the family.

12. *Do* make sure all medical procedures are explained.

13. *Do* explain the victim's right to privacy during examinations; also, explain the right to have a parent present (if desired by the victim).

14. *Do* make certain instructions are written when the patient is discharged; and do encourage follow-up.

## DON'T

1. *Don't* project your own feelings onto the victim or family.

2. *Don't* take sides regarding the sexual abuse by showing anger or discussing punishment.

3. *Don't* allow the child to feel alone or at fault.

4. *Don't* criticize the victim or his or her family.

5. *Don't* offer unsolicited advice to victim or family.

6. *Don't* allow the victim or family to think that disclosures regarding sexual abuse can be kept confidential.

7. *Don't* break any confidences of patient or family unless they relate to abuse.

8. *Don't* tell the patient or family what they must/must not do regarding legal aspects of the abuse.

9.  *Don't* discuss the particulars with visitors or hospital personnel unless making a report to authorities.

10. *Don't* advise the victim or family as to how to handle pregnancy.

11. *Don't* leave the victim with a stranger, i.e., someone the *nurse* doesn't know and trust.

## Legal Management

Child sexual abuse is governed by both criminal and civil statutes. The criminal court has jurisdiction over the perpetrator while the civil system has jurisdiction over the child. In other words, jurisdiction over the child remains in the province of the parents and juvenile court.

Federal and state laws govern the reporting of child sexual abuse. Since the regulations tend to vary from state to state, it is advisable for professionals to obtain copies of current laws governing reporting. Most states mandate that professionals report cases of child sexual abuse. However, pedophilic and child pornographic activities, plus sexual exploitation of children for purposes of prostitution and pedophilic activities, whether mandated or not, should always be reported. (See Table 6-3.)

If there is any suspicion that the parents of the victim are not assuming a protective role toward the child, a report can be made simultaneously to the police and to C.P.S. (Child Protective Services). For example, if a parent is participating in or encouraging his or her child to engage in sexual or pornograhic activities, that parent should be reported to Child Protective Services. If the pedophile lives in the home and the parent refuses to evict him, C.P.S. will remove the child to shelter or foster care. In some instances, the pedophile is also an incestuous offender who may be abusing his own child.

# Table 6-3: Sample Sexual Abuse Report

                                                    Date _____ Time _____

                                                    Therapist_____

Client/Patient's Name_____

D.O.B._____

Mother's Name _____

Tel _____        S.S.# _____

Address _____

Father's Name_____

Tel _____        S.S.# _____

Address _____

Child's Current Residence _____

*History:* Nine-year-old Mary brought by Fay, natural mother, to Cedarville Rape and Abuse Counseling Center re: allegations of long-term sexual abuse by natural father. On eve of _____ _____, Mother reports Mary informed her, "Daddy put his pee-pee in me down below and squirted white stuff." Mother states Mary told friend, Jane Lester, about the abuse and friend advised Mary to tell her Mother. Mother states Mary told her, "Daddy has been doing this a lot." Mary reports Dad first "touched me down below" in 1st grade. She states, "He came to my room at night at 11:00 p.m. just after Mommy left for work."

She further stated, "Sometimes he lay next to me and rubbed his pee-pee between my legs. Once he tried to put it in my mouth but I told him not to." Mary said Dad told her he would leave her in the woods if she told anyone. She was able to pinpoint two exact times when sexual abuse occurred—on her eighth birthday (attempted oral sex, approximately 11:00 p.m.) and the day before New Year's Eve this year (manual rubbing of genitals, "late at night"). She claims she could pinpoint first date because "I was sad he did that on my birthday." She recalls second date because "Daddy had been to a party and was drunk and I thought he'd leave me alone." Father currently is in home; also, two younger siblings—Josh, 6, and Cindy, 2.

*Assessment of Risk*: Apparently protective mother currently in shock. Appears willing to leave home or have offender leave. Is willing to make police report. Has support system in town (parents, _____, with whom she can reside, and friends).

*Medical Information*: No current reports.

*Action*; Police called from Center. Officer _____ interviewed family and will see alleged offender at work. CPS notified and investigator, _____, will make home visit. Family referred to _____ for sexual abuse exam. Follow-up appointment made at Center for _____.

---

*Follow-up Data*: On _____, CPS investigator _____, called to state home visit made. Father out of home. Children with mother. Mary's exam at _____ hospital revealed no physical signs of sexual abuse/no genital trauma or discharge. Hymen intact. Wet prep from vagina negative for sperm.

*Note*: Essential data in the above report includes:

1) Names, addresses, and telephone numbers of key contacts

2) Full details of sexual abuse with identification of each informant

3) Precise dates of sexual abuse

4) Assessment of risk for victim

5) Family situation including presence of younger siblings at home

6) Actions taken to ensure safety of child

7) Assessment of support for family

8) Provisions for follow-up

Some states levy penalties against professionals who fail to report sexual abuse. These penalties range from fines to imprisonment to both. Usually, however, even if an investigation reveals that abuse is not occurring, there is no penalty for reporting suspected abuse. If, on the other hand, a professional does not report suspected abuse and the child later is harmed, the professional may be sued under civil or criminal penalties.

In general, professionals have been reluctant to report child sexual abuse. In some cases, they fear retaliation from the perpetrator or parents. There also is fear that little will be accomplished if a report is registered. An additional factor is ignorance of laws on what types of activities must be reported. Finally, professionals want to avoid legal entanglements whenever possible.

The responsible professional informs parents of victims that a report will be made and that the professional is available for supportive follow-up. Keep an accurate set of records for use in court. All documentation should be factual and descriptive. Labels and interpretations should be avoided. Records should include drawings, evidence of physical trauma, descriptions of general appearance, attitudes and behaviors of victims and parents, and statements by the family regarding what actually occurred. (See Tables 6-4 and 6-5.)

Despite the fact that child sexual abuse is against the law, legal action often is a lengthy, frustrating and fruitless process for parents and children alike. One authority stated that the chances for a pedophile "to be caught, convicted and serve a prison sentence are like the chances of being hit by lightning."

# Table 6-4: Steps in the Legal Process in Child Sexual Abuse Cases*

1. Sexual abuse disclosed

2. Police called

3. Sexual assault/crimes officer sees family for report. (In incest cases, Child Protective Services notified to assess child's situation. May remove child from home depending on whether or not offender leaves.) Medical services/counseling recommended

4. Police detective from sex crimes unit interviews victim

5. Police file with County Attorney

6. County Attorney files complaint

7. Arraignment

8. Preliminary hearing in municipal court. Offender may/may not be out of jail on own recognizance

9. Information filed against defendant

10. Arraignment in superior court

11. Superior court trial

---

* For situations where offender pleads not guilty/does not plea bargain.

# Table 6-5: Legal Process in Incest/Sexual Abuse Cases

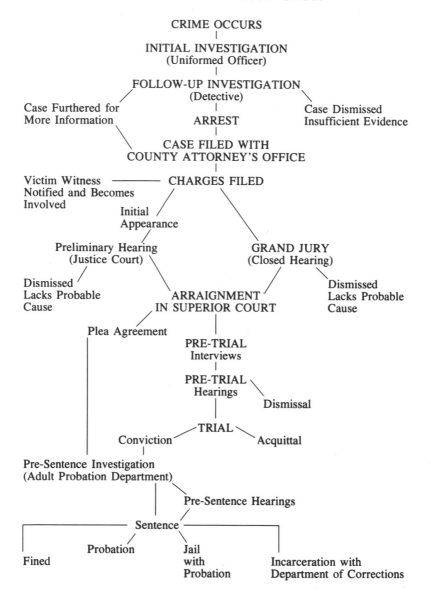

CRIME OCCURS

INITIAL INVESTIGATION
(Uniformed Officer)

FOLLOW-UP INVESTIGATION
(Detective)

Case Furthered for
More Information

Case Dismissed
Insufficient Evidence

ARREST

CASE FILED WITH
COUNTY ATTORNEY'S OFFICE

Victim Witness
Notified and Becomes
Involved

CHARGES FILED

Initial
Appearance

Preliminary Hearing
(Justice Court)

GRAND JURY
(Closed Hearing)

Dismissed
Lacks Probable
Cause

ARRAIGNMENT
IN SUPERIOR COURT

Dismissed
Lacks Probable
Cause

Plea Agreement

PRE-TRIAL
Interviews

PRE-TRIAL
Hearings

Dismissal

TRIAL

Conviction

Acquittal

Pre-Sentence Investigation
(Adult Probation Department)

Pre-Sentence Hearings

Sentence

Fined

Probation

Jail
with
Probation

Incarceration with
Department of Corrections

In 1981 in California, there were 50,000 children known to have been sexually molested. Despite these staggering figures, fully 62% of the offenders who were convicted for child molestation received sentences of probation. The average length of time of imprisonment for those sentenced to incarceration was 3.5 years. Thirty-eight states have no laws against child rape.

Some professionals believe that it is important for parents to be warned of the frustrations involved in the court process. Court delays can be endless and plea bargaining is the likely outcome. During such delays, many children begin to experience a wide variety of psychological and psychosomatic complaints. Nightmares are a common occurrence, along with headaches and stomach discomfort. The child's social adjustment may be in jeopardy along with his or her academic progress. Some parents seek the services of a counselor or therapist for their children to relieve the victim's anxiety during waiting periods, and to prepare him or her for the ordeal of giving direct testimony in the offender's presence. Other parents decide it is wisest to discourage their child from testifying, in which case the prosecutor often is forced to drop all charges against the perpetrator.

Ultimately, the child must decide whether or not to testify. Going through the court process can be beneficial in validating the child's credibility. It often serves to establish concrete identification of who was wronged and who was to blame for the wrongdoing. One child who did testify stated that she felt as if she were vomiting and "getting rid of all the anger." Another young victim stated that after her court appearance she felt as if a thousand pounds were lifted from her. On the other hand, some children who show extreme anxiety over the court process should not be encouraged to testify.

It has become increasingly customary to seek objective information regarding medical and/or psychological particulars in cases of child sexual abuse by requiring professional workers to furnish testimony. To minimize trauma to the victim by eliminating

his or her direct testimony, child advocates are encouraging
surrogate testimony by social workers, counselors, nurses and
physicians. If a professional is required to testify, she or he may
find the following guidelines useful:

- Be prepared. Review any notes carefully and bring to court
  any relevant documents that have been subpoenaed.

- Answer all questions directly and honestly. It is preferable
  to respond, ''I don't know,'' than to take sides or form
  irrelevant interpretations.

- Avoid the use of jargon and present all facts briefly and
  concisely.

- Avoid distracting mannerisms (such as chewing gum while
  testifying).

- Listen carefully to the questions posed and avoid ''snap''
  or quick answers. Take time to think.

- Answer only the question asked. Do not volunteer
  information.

- Stop immediately if the judge interrupts you or when an
  attorney objects to a question.

- Give positive and definite answers whenever possible.
  Avoid saying, ''I think,'' or ''I believe.''

- Don't ask the judge for advice or an opinion. Do not ask
  him whether or not you must answer a certain question.

- Never argue with the judge or the attorneys.

With regard to incestuous abuse in particular, there are a few additional issues to consider in terms of case management. It is especially important in incest situations to interview victims separately from other family members. The father may be entrenched in denial—or he may have threatened his daughter. The mother may be so invested in maintaining an intact family that she, too, has frightened her daughter into showing reluctance to disclose the facts.

In incestuous families, there usually are other children in the home and it is the interviewer's responsibility to ascertain whether these children are, or have been, victims of abuse. With incest cases, Child Protective Services often becomes involved to ensure the ongoing safety of all children in the family.

Professionals should be aware of three pitfalls encountered when dealing with incest. The first pitfall relates to the tendency among professionals to deny or minimize incest because of the horror the very word seems to elicit in most people. Time and again experienced clinicians have been remiss in detecting, identifying and reporting incest. These same professionals readily manage rape and extrafamilial molestation cases with expertise. Hence, it is important to remember how prevalent incest is and how rarely children lie about molestation. The clues usually are there and the professional should be alert to their presence.

A second pitfall concerns the need for medical, educational and other professionals to stabilize and objectify their own attitudes before attempting to deal with incest families. Even experienced professionals have found themselves expressing strong negative judgments and even overt anger toward offenders during initial interviews. Anger also is a common reaction in interviewers when they encounter a denying mother. In order to best serve their clients, it is important for all professionals to be aware of their feelings and to monitor them appropriately. If the professional can remember his or her ultimate goal, i.e., to gather information and to ensure protection of the victim, it will become easier to keep personal values in abeyance. Also, the professional must remember that, since he or she may be the first authority figure the family encounters, the initial interview will set the tone for all subsequent interactions an offender, his spouse, and victim will have with professionals. Finally, it is important to view the family humanely, realizing that incest families are disturbed and very much in need of help and guidance.

Legally, incest is a criminal act requiring the same case management guidelines that apply to all other types of sexual abuse. Many states do not have a comprehensive incest treatment program such as Giarretto's. Police and court proceedings are similar to those outlined earlier for cases of pedophilia and child rape. There is no automatic plea bargain procedure nor is there a mandated court order to place families in therapy programs. Because of the absence of a systematic approach, offenders guilty of similar forms of abuse often receive widely varying sentences.

Despite the negative aspects of court involvement, professionals should report all cases of suspected incest. Some professionals are reluctant to report incest because they know that the child might suffer by having to testify—or because they believe sex offenders might be murdered if they are convicted and sent to join the general prison population. In addition, professionals sometimes react to the frustrations inherent in the legal system when dealing with incestuous families. Incest offenders often are not convicted because, at the last moment, the child has refused to testify—either out of loyalty to the offender or because the mother has convinced her or him that conviction would not be in the family's best interests.

Despite possible negative outcomes, professionals must remember that their role is to follow ethical and legal guidelines. Incest may be a frustrating, complicated and value-laden issue, but it is also illegal; and in most situations the consequences to victims are devastating.

# 7

# Prevention and Detection

The cycle of child sexual abuse can be stopped but we must have stronger, more consistent laws and we must educate ourselves and our children about this devastating epidemic. Professional workers, especially, should pay attention to high risk families and should be alert to possibilities that abuse is or has been occurring. It is the responsibility of educators, physicians, nurses and counselors to watch for behavioral clues of sexual abuse, particularly in high risk populations.

## The Educator's Role

Teachers and school social workers have a key role in preventing, identifying and responding to the problem of child sexual abuse. Teachers spend up to eight hours per day with children in their charge. They are in a position to know the child, his or her habits, patterns and responses better than anyone else outside the home and thus are best able to detect behavioral and emotional changes indicative of abuse problems. To young children, especially, the teacher symbolizes both authority and protection and elicits trust and respect. Many Child Protective Service caseworkers report that a large number of their abuse referrals originate from caring and discerning school personnel.

Above all else, educators must possess knowledge about child sexual abuse, the enormity of the problem, its devastating effects and the clues for its identification. Educators need to know the main indicators and signs of abuse. They should:

- Pay attention to the child whose grades suddenly plummet

- Monitor the behavior of the youngster who becomes withdrawn for no discernible cause or whose peer relationships suddenly decay

- Watch for unexplained irritability or crying spells

- Find out why a youngster is staying late after school or habitually arriving early

- Be aware of the child who refuses to participate in physical education classes or to take showers with peers

Teachers who suspect that a child is being abused should take her or him aside for an informal talk. A teacher can create an atmosphere of openness and trust by showing a general interest in the child and by assuring her or him of the teacher's availability and interest. If the child does disclose abuse, the following points need to be established:

- The victim was not to blame

- Disclosure of abuse is right and proper

- The victim is no longer alone

- The matter must be placed in the hands of legal authorities in order to help the victim

Some teachers ask if they should let children know about the mandate to report abuse before the youngsters make a full disclosure. Most professionals agree that it is, indeed, advisable to do so whenever possible. In that way, full trust is maintained and you, the teacher, have ample opportunity to explain fully why you are duty-bound to make a report. Educators are required to report abuse for the following reasons:

- The law has been broken

- The victim and his or her siblings must be protected from further abuse

- The victim's family is in need of help

Educators need to know the law on reporting child abuse and neglect in their region. They also need to be fully aware of school policy for reporting suspected abuse, plus any guidelines for school personnel to follow in reporting abuse. If the child makes only a partial disclosure, or in the event that there has been no disclosure, you still must report suspected abuse. In 1982, there were 37 states mandating schools and/or school personnel to report suspected cases of child abuse and neglect. School personnel in the remainder of the states fall under the federal mandate for "any person" to report suspected abuse. Every state, with the exception of Oklahoma, provides immunity from criminal and civil liability for anyone who makes such a report in good faith.

Teachers should never contact parents on their own initiative, but should go through the appropriate channels. In most schools, teachers refer knowledge or suspicion of child abuse to school counselors who then notify Child Protective Services. Once a report is made, the teacher should be available to the child and her or his family for emotional support. The teacher can serve as a resource for over-stressed parents and can refer to appropriate school personnel for follow-up and full assessment.

Educators should provide students with a forum for discussion of values and goals. An atmosphere of openness will facilitate disclosure of fears and anxieties. Children should be taught to respect their bodies and to protect themselves from physical and emotional harm; teachers can incorporate this information into daily activities through use of established school programs such as Carol A. Plummer's *Preventing Sexual Abuse: Activities and Strategies For Those Working With Children and Adolescents* (Learning Publications Inc., Holmes Beach, Florida, 1984). One teacher uses recess as an opportunity to model and to help children role play assertive versus passive responses to aggression. (See Table 7-1.)

Teachers should be encouraged to take the initiative in helping their school district institute new educational programs. Fortunately, rising concern about the problem of child sexual abuse has resulted in the development of many excellent materials for teaching about this subject. Each school should have a child abuse prevention team composed of the school counselor, school nurse and psychologist. The psychologist's function is to be available as a resource for the classroom teacher, to monitor and assess suspected abuse situations, and to educate the staff through in-service training, distribution of handouts and recommendations for the purchase of child abuse prevention materials. Each school should have a child abuse manual outlining the types of child abuse, laws governing abuse, mandated reporting, indicators and signs of abuse, and specific procedures to follow.

According to the Education Commission of the States' Report #85, only a small percentage of state departments of education and school districts have policies and procedures for reporting abuse. Eighty-four percent of the state departments of education and 56% of the largest school districts in each state have no guidelines for reporting. Only ten percent of the largest private schools in each state have policies to report. Ideally, a policy should inform school personnel both of legal and professional obligations and of laws governing immunity from civil and criminal liability when suspected abuse has been reported in good faith.

# Table 7-1: Issues to Include When Teaching Children About Child Sexual Abuse

| Goal | Essential Points to Include |
|---|---|
| • ABUSE CAN OCCUR.<br>To alert children to the possibility of sexual abuse | • Most people treat children well and can be trusted<br><br>• Sometimes adults (even relatives) or older children touch children where they shouldn't. Adults may touch a child's private parts (penis, vagina, breast etc.) even though they know it is wrong |
| • NO ONE SHOULD TOUCH A CHILD'S PRIVATE PARTS.<br>To teach children that their bodies belong to them and that no one has the right to touch them in any way that makes them uncomfortable | • No one has the right to touch anyone (child or adult) anywhere that makes that person uncomfortable and/or to touch their private parts |
| • "YELL AND TELL."<br>To advise children on how to handle potential sexual abuse | • If someone tries to touch a child's privates or entrap her/him, the child should run away and scream for help |
| • REPORT ANY ABUSE.<br>To instruct children as to what to do if sexual abuse occurs | • A child who has been sexually abused should tell a trusted adult immediately (parent, teacher, minister, other). If the adult does not believe the child and/or take action, the child should tell another adult and proceed until she/he is believed |
| • CHILDREN ARE NEVER AT FAULT.<br>To reassure children in the event that sexual abuse occurs | • Children must *never* think they are to blame when sexually abused by an adult or older child; the older person is the one to blame. Thousands of children are abused every year by selfish, unthinking people; it is the victim's responsibility to report such abuse so it can be stopped. Victims should not feel guilty or afraid. |

Local educators should be aware of, and help to institute, a sexual abuse prevention curriculum in their schools. Several appropriate prevention programs are listed in this text under Appendix A: Resources.

Finally, the services of rape crisis and sexual abuse centers should be utilized for presentation of periodic in-service training workshops to heighten awareness and knowledge of school personnel. These agencies are usually also prepared to do presentations for parent groups.

## The Parent's Role

Parents have a major responsibility to teach their youngsters about sexual abuse, safety and self-defense. Imparting information about body parts, appropriate and inappropriate touching and self-protection are part of good parenting and can begin at any age. (See Tables 7-2 and 7-3.)

Parents may start by teaching their children the correct names for the parts of her or his body. Learning the correct terms diffuses anxiety about the genitals and facilitates accurate reporting in the event that abuse occurs. One five-year-old girl told her mother quite simply, "Joe has been touching my vagina."

Children should be taught the differences between appropriate and inappropriate touching (or "good" and "bad") touching. Parents can be encouraged to help their children describe and label the different types of touching that they have experienced—including affectionate parental hugs and kisses, punitive spankings and sibling wrestling matches. Children should be introduced to the notion of inappropriate touching of their bodies and advised that no one has the right to touch their genitals or to touch them in ways that make them feel uncomfortable. Children need to know that adults (any adult, including relatives and close family friends) sometimes make mistakes and touch children where they should not. It will be helpful to provide an open atmosphere in which children may ask questions and also disclose anything that may have happened in the past.

Parents need to tell their children to talk with them if anyone touches them in any way that causes discomfort. Parents are encouraged to be clear in specifying what they mean; i.e., "No adult has the right to touch your penis." Children should be advised that if they feel unable to report abuse to their parents they should tell someone else—a teacher, a minister, a family friend. If that person does not believe the child, she or he should tell someone else.

Parents need to teach their children when to say *No*. Unfortunately, most youngsters are trained to obey their elders and to trust all adults. One incestuous father molested five of his six daughters. When the sixth child was questioned, it was learned that she escaped victimization because she was the only one of the children who said "No!" to her father. We need to teach children to make a scene, to create trouble for anyone who is a potential offender, to "Yell and Tell" (as one prevention program is called).

Some authorities suggest that parents play a game of "What if?" with children, to help them rehearse how they would handle the approach of a pedophile.* Children are very literal and tend to have difficulties generalizing; therefore, advice regarding specific situations is most helpful to them. Examples of appropriate "what if?" situations are:

1.  What if a man asks you to help him find his lost puppy?

2.  What if your ball rolls into a stranger's yard?

3.  What if Mom is late picking you up from school and the schoolyard becomes deserted? What would you do?

4.  What if a strange person tells you he or she has been sent to take you to your mother, who is in the hospital?

---

* Sanford, L. *The Silent Children: A Parent's Guide to the Prevention of Child Sexual Abuse*. New York: Doubleday, 1980.

5.  What if a stranger offers you candy, video games, money (or whatever else has special appeal)?

6.  What if you become lost (a) in a city? (b) on a camping trip?

Children should be taught to protect themselves by running from strangers, by screaming, by seeking help from adults in the vicinity and by being verbally assertive with sexual offenders. Remember that educating children does not increase fears. On the contrary, it instills in them a sense of self-worth and strength derived from the knowledge that they can develop control over their own destinies.

## Table 7-2: Assertiveness for Children: Overview of Important Points

1.  Assertive Rights of Children Relative to Self-Protection

    A.  Children have the right to express their thoughts, feelings, opinions and ideas.

    B.  Children have the right to protect themselves from harm.

    C.  Children have the right to:

        • Be treated with respect as human beings

        • Say "no" to adults or peers when they feel uncomfortable or threatened

        • Protect themselves and their bodies

        • Be believed

2. Assertive Behavior Involves

   A. Equalizing the balance of power and expressing individual rights, needs, wants, feelings and opinions

   B. Both the "what" and "how" of self-expression

   C. Both words and body language (eye contact, erect posture, and clear and audible tone of voice)

3. Differences Between Assertive, Passive and Aggressive Behaviors

   A. Assertive behavior is prompted by honesty and directness. Examples of assertive behavior are, "No, I will not do that," "Leave me alone," and "I feel threatened and am going to report this."

   B. Passive behavior is prompted by shyness, low self-concept and uncertainty. Examples of passive behavior are, "Well, I'm not sure about this at all and will have to think about it," and, "I don't think that I want to go with you but maybe it would be O.K."

   C. Aggressive behavior is prompted by anger and revenge. Examples of aggressive behavior are, "You creep, don't you dare talk to me or I'll hit you," and, "I'll kill you if you come near me." (Note: In general, assertive behavior is recommended. There are times, however, when it is appropriate and necessary for children to behave aggressively with a potential assailant. Unfortunately, aggressive behavior can elicit aggressive responses from the recipient and hence should be avoided whenever possible.)

Parents should be aware of where their children are—and with whom. Are they hitching rides? Are they spending too much time at YMCA's, local swimming pools, arcades, bus depots, bowling alleys, bike shops, school yards or parks? Parents should evaluate the *WHERE, WHY,* and *WITH WHOM* of their children's daily activities and get to know their children's leaders in Scouts, Big Brothers, church groups, recreation clubs or boys' clubs.

One million, eight hundred thousand children are reported missing each year. Approximately 100,000 are taken by non-custodial parents. At least 50,000 others simply disappear. In the latter group, the fatality rate is very high and many, if not most, of these abducted children become victims of sexual abuse. Parents can help to combat this problem by organizing parent communication groups to disseminate information and to coordinate support for educational, treatment and law enforcement programs.

Ken Wooden, author of ''Child Lures: A Guide to Prevent Abduction,'' lists nine lures commonly used by molesters:

1. Affection (feigning love for the child or demonstrating kindness)

2. Assistance (asking help from potential child victims)

3. Authority (posing as policemen or clergy to elicit trust from children)

4. Bribery (offering the child monetary or social rewards for sexual favors)

5. Ego (promising victims fame through commercial endeavors such as modeling)

6. Emergency (claiming to be helping the family in crisis situations)

7. Games and fun (offering entertainment and amusement to potential victims)

8. Employment (offering jobs in exchange for sex)

9. Threats (frightening or blackmailing children)

Parents should educate their youngsters about these lures and encourage them to report any suspicious incidents.

Latchkey children also constitute a high-risk population for victimization by sex offenders. The number of latchkey children in the United States appears to have increased dramatically in recent years. Currently, an estimated two to four million children care for themselves without adult supervision before and after school and during vacations. Twenty to fifty thousand of these children are preschoolers.

The dramatic increase in the number of latchkey children in the last decade can be attributed to a variety of social changes. Our high national divorce rate has resulted in an increase in working mothers and single parent families. Inflation has contributed to the problem by forcing housewives into the world of work (two-thirds of mothers of school-age children currently are employed) and by deterring limited income families from availing themselves of day care services. Finally, the social and physical mobility experienced in recent years has contributed to alienation and the breakdown of the extended family which, in former times, provided built-in support or baby-sitting for the now isolated nuclear family.

Fortunately, many communities are beginning to seek creative solutions to the problems posed by latchkey children. The city of Houston, Texas, now has a hotline, called Chatters, to provide telephone counseling and advice to latchkey children and their families. Corvallis, Oregon, publishes "Latchkey Notes," a newsletter offering information and support to the community. Johnson County, Kansas, has devised and implemented a school curriculum called, "I'm in Charge," to assist families with self-care children. The curriculum is accompanied by a film, "Lord of the Locks," which teaches survival skills to the children. Camp Fire offers, "I Can Do It," a survival training course for school age children, and the Boy Scouts has prepared a manual on self-care and survival for latchkey children.

## Table 7-3: Safety Tips to Protect Children from Sexual Abuse

1. Never leave young children alone at home. If a child has to be left alone in an emergency, instruct that child not to answer the telephone or door to anyone.

2. Instruct children as to how to handle any obscene telephone calls: a) hang up immediately or blow a whistle into the phone, and b) report the call to parents.

3. Find a trusted neighbor to whom the child can report in an emergency. Make sure that the child knows the location of the neighbor's home and telephone number.

4. Make sure children know how to locate parents/relatives/ trusted friends by having them memorize telephone numbers and addresses to use in the event of an emergency. Parents should familiarize their children with the family's general daily schedule (shopping days, place and days of employment, favorite restaurants etc.).

5. Help establish E-Houses (Emergency Houses) locally. Participants in the E-House project agree to place a poster board with the large letter E in their windows whenever they are at home. In the event that she/he becomes lost or frightened, a child can find safety at any E House.

6. Always know the who-where-why-with whom concerning the whereabouts of minor children.

7. Get full background knowledge on Boy Scout leaders, boys' clubs, sports directors and babysitters.

8. Have children use a buddy system when walking to or from school, when playing arcade games and when participating in after-school events.

9. Instruct children on how to conduct themselves in public: a) avoid strangers, b) avoid deserted areas and short-cuts such as vacant or parking lots, c) walk near the curb facing traffic, d) reverse direction if a car pulls up next to the child, and e) "yell and tell" if anyone approaches.

10. Instruct children not to tell anyone about family plans and daily routines.

11. Teach children about child sexual abuse, inappropriate and appropriate touching (by strangers or relatives), and what to do in the event that child sexual abuse occurs.

12. Use specific techniques of assertiveness training and "what if" games to instruct children about self-protection; i.e., teach children how to maintain personal control of their bodies, and then practice their responses to questions such as, "What if a stranger said that he found money and offered to give you some of it?"

13. Believe any child who reports child sexual abuse and take appropriate action. Make sure the child knows that a) she/he did the correct thing by telling about the abuse, b) she/he is not responsible or guilty, and c) she/he is not alone.

We are witnessing the growth of grass-roots and community based programs to diminish the risks for children who lack adult supervision for extended periods of time each day. New programs include child care cooperatives, hotlines, before and after school programs and modified employee work schedules allowing for flexible hours to enable parents to meet their children's needs more adequately.

It is important for parents to be aware of both the normal stages of sex play for children and the indicators of possible child sexual abuse. Between the ages of two and three, children normally show an interest in the physical differences between the sexes. Girls may attempt to urinate standing up. At about age four, there may be a heightened interest in the bathroom activities of others, along with a demand for self-privacy. Children may touch their genitals when they are excited or under stress. Games such as ''Show and Tell'' or ''Doctor and Nurse'' are commonly played. Interest may diminish at five, then be renewed at about six or seven with possible mutual investigation, giggling and game playing. By age eight, there may be less sex exploration but joking and whispering continues. At nine or ten, children often begin to share sex information.

Obviously, children vary in their interest in sex and bodily functions. The important point to remember is that it is perfectly normal for young children to manifest a curiosity about their bodies and the bodies of other children and adults. Game playing, looking, joking and sex exploration are part of the normal developmental stages in prepubescent youngsters.

Parents can expect their children to pass through these normal stages with variations depending on the particular level of development, peer contacts and personality. What parents should be alert to are the signs and clues that indicate the possible existence of problems:

- Sudden withdrawal.

- Preoccupation with the genitals

- Poor peer relations

- Aggressive or regressed behavior

- Unexplained fears

- Sleeping disorders

- Persistent psychosomatic complaints

If the child does tell a parent that she or he has been sexually abused, the parent should first find a private place to talk with the victim and determine exactly what occurred. A parent should not express shock, anger or disapproval, but should explain first that the parent is sorry about what happened and that he or she is there to protect the victim. Parents are advised to:

- Give plenty of reassurance and support.

- Believe what the child tells you.

- Contact your physician if the child has been injured.

- Report the abuse to the police or local child sexual assault center.

- Respect your child's privacy by disclosing the abuse only to involved professionals or the victim's family.

- Consider follow-up supportive counseling which is recommended.

Concerning the parental role in prevention of child sexual abuse, one final issue merits attention. Parents should be aware of their own sexual feelings towards their children and their children's sexual feelings towards them. In *The Broken Taboo: Sex In The Family*, Justice and Justice present advice regarding behaviors related to sexual feelings between parent and child. These authors stress the importance of avoiding daily habits that could cause sexual overstimulation. Among situations of which parents are cautioned to be aware are: sleeping arrangements; nudity in the home; sexual aspects of contact games between parents and children; provocative aspects of adult-to-adult sexual contacts in front of the child; and verbal exhibitionism, which can manifest itself in a number of ways. For example, parents should never discuss adult sexual relationships with, or in the presence of, their children. Sometimes the line between healthy manifestation of needed affection and subtle exploitation of feelings can be a thin one. Parents have the responsibility of respecting that line, and of upholding the integrity of the child-parent relationship.

There is little question that we need stronger legislation to stop child sexual abuse. Interested citizens, whether professionally involved or not, can demand that their congressmen and senators introduce new and stronger laws.

In the end, preventive measures will involve a coordinated and interdisciplinary effort of social workers (Child Protective Services), health and educational workers, the legal system and the police. The problem requires a multi-faceted approach involving increased public awareness, education, early identification, parenting programs, supportive interventions, improved therapeutic intervention strategies and—above all—new, more effective legislation.

# 8

# Resources and Referrals

While interest in child sexual abuse has grown in the last few years, professionals are still markedly unaware of, and unskilled and untrained in the area of child abuse. There is widespread misunderstanding of the dynamics of abuse, the characteristics found in abusing families and individuals, and of the varying treatment modalities currently in use. A 1982 survey of 64 social service and mental health agencies in the Phoenix metropolitan area, for example, indicated that only a few professionals were interested in, or aware of, the magnitude of the problem. Workers at most agencies minimized the extent of abuse and the resultant trauma for families. If abuse was not a direct part of the presenting problem, it was played down or ignored. If agency personnel believed abuse to be current or relevant, they automatically referred it to Child Protective Services, the police or the local rape crisis center—without follow-up and without consideration of the quality of services.

In an area as sensitive as sexual abuse, where families typically are in crisis and where involvement with law enforcement is often mandated, the necessity for trained counselors cannot be minimized (see Appendix A for list of resources). Families complain about the lack of understanding and consistency in services. Many state that they receive incomplete, inadequate or contradictory advice from different counselors, police and Child Protective Services workers. Much of this inconsistency stems from ignorance on the part of the various professionals involved.

For a family seeking skilled services from a counselor on child sexual abuse, and for a professional worker wishing to make referrals for such services, there are no easy answers. Finding a qualified therapist is a difficult task. Unfortunately, training and expertise alone do not guarantee quality and objectivity. The field of child sexual abuse counseling attracts some professionals who themselves have therapeutic issues with which to deal. The subject of sexual abuse is sufficiently titillating to draw therapists who have hidden, usually unconscious, reasons for choosing this specialty. In addition, some therapists unconsciously defend against the behavioral problems they purport to treat. Due to their lack of objectivity and defenses, these professionals often do irrevocable harm to their clients.

In order to increase and identify reputable resources, local areas would do well to compile a directory of agencies and therapists specializing in child sexual abuse. Such a directory should list names of individuals and services along with their qualifications, education, years of experience, particular expertise (group, family, relationship, children, adolescents, women molested as children, offenders), fees, specialized modalities (gestalt, behavioral management, reality therapy etc.), and type of therapy (long-term, short-term, crisis).

In addition to compiling an up-to-date resource directory, community agencies should encourage staff members to attend regional and local workshops and training events on child abuse. In-service training within agencies should be a requirement of the job. Also, professionals can increase their expertise, referral systems and support structures through monthly inter-agency meetings that focus on sharing research materials and giving/ receiving feedback regarding therapeutic approaches, techniques and modalities. Inter-agency councils and sexual abuse committees also facilitate growth and learning.

In the absence of resource directories and adequate referral systems, professionals should be cautious in making referrals to therapists. Local rape crisis centers can be a good resource, but all too often they hire paraprofessionals and focus on crisis intervention strategies only. Many early rape crisis and sexual assault centers were grass roots operations that have developed through volunteer efforts, with little community support or federal and state guidelines to follow. As the need for services increased, some of these centers have expanded while making few internal changes. As a result, some of them may lack both professionalism and qualified staff, and many of their policies and procedures may remain antiquated. Nonetheless, as emergency centers for initial one-on-one contact with crisis clients, they remain a viable resource. Unfortunately, despite our need for professional expertise, most therapists simply are inadequately trained to deal with incestuous families and pedophiles. Cases of intra- and extrafamilial molestation involve complex issues that necessitate specialized training and considerable experience among clinicians.

Clients should be apprised of these difficulties within the profession and should be encouraged to be assertive and knowledgeable when seeking appropriate therapeutic interventions. A client has the right to directly request information regarding the training, expertise, education and experience of prospective therapists and to seek alternate treatment if not satisfied with the services received. Clients who are informed and assertive will do much to upgrade and increase services to the victims of sexual abuse. Professionals who assist their communities to be better informed on the problem of sexual abuse and the need for better services to victims will make a significant contribution to prevention, intervention and recovery efforts.

# AFTERWORD

## The Story of Uncle Jess:
## A Personal Account by a Survivor

By Pat Lucadano

The following fictionalized account of incest highlights the feelings and reactions of child victims and provides an excellent example of material which can be used for bibliotherapy. The author describes the process of writing her story as follows:

> The story is fiction—at least as far as the details are concerned. I had no uncle; my father lived until I was in my forties. There is no family member, living or dead, to be disturbed by it. In a far deeper sense, however, it is not fiction. The feelings and the motives are authentic. The story rolled out of my typewriter one morning as if it had a life of its own. I feel that it is a gift and I want to share it. It has been a great satisfaction to me as I have seen it help others.

> Pat Lucadano

The year I was nine, my father was killed in an industrial accident. My mother sold our home in Chicago and moved my brother Bobby and me to Barrington to be near her mother and her brother Jess.

I took the loss of my father very hard and adjusted poorly to the move to Barrington. For a long time I felt that my mother and my brother were disloyal to Daddy by getting on with their lives. It seemed so wrong to me to see my mother involved with the Methodist Church and the Ladies Auxiliary at the local hospital. It hurt me to see Bobby playing ball with the neighborhood kids every chance he got.

I was lonely and refused to make friends, refused to get involved in any of the activities of the neighborhood or at Sunday School. I moped. I sat for long hours staring into the fireplace, trying to remember Daddy's face. I was panicked because his memory was fading. I longed for the strong man-feel of him, like clinging to an oak tree. I needed my Daddy.

Uncle Jess was very close to my mother. He spent a lot of time at our house, when we weren't at his house, where he lived with Granny Ida. He did odd jobs around our house and he helped with chores. He seemed to be part of the family, right from the start, and was the one bright spot in an otherwise bleak stretch of time. Uncle Jess hugged. He brought presents. He whistled. He whittled. He told shaggy dog stories and "knock knock" jokes. Slowly I began to follow him around as I allowed my grief to ease ever so slightly.

One day, in the dining room of the old house we lived in, Uncle Jess grabbed me in his bear hug and swung me up to the ceiling. I laughed, because I loved being swung high, and hung on. When he brought me down he kept me in his embrace. I didn't want to let go of the man-feel, I wanted to cling, and I couldn't believe what his hand was doing beneath my skirt. It was a "bad thing," and I stayed very still, trying not to know that one of the most important adults in my life was doing it. I was incapable of moving. I stared at the corner where the paisley wallpaper met the dark walnut paneling. There was a knot in the wood, and I stared at it, memorizing it, rigidly not thinking. He moved his hand away, and then I could move. I was so embarrassed I wanted to die! I didn't know how to look him in the eye after I had let him do that to me. Uncle Jess couldn't meet my eye, either, but he said "Let this be our little secret, Janey. Nobody has to know." I would have let wild horses pull me apart before I told anyone!

It was more than a week later that I found myself alone in the cellar with Uncle Jess. He hugged me naturally, but I stiffened; I knew what was coming. Uncle Jess was still Uncle Jess, though, and I loved him. I felt guilty and ashamed at the same time. I had let him fondle me before; I had said nothing; and it seemed to me now that I had no right to say "No." All I could do was concentrate fiercely on not thinking, while my most private parts were invaded. I stared at the woodbox, concentrated on the nails in the corner of it, smelled the odors of mustiness and fresh wood, watched dust motes dance in the sunbeam shining through the small, high window. I watched our cat stroll by outside the window, listened to water gurgle through the pipes over my head. Anything—anything at all—not to have to know what was going on in those nethermost parts, not to know the intense pleasure my body was feeling, nor the shame of it. I felt so alone and apart from my family at that moment. I felt bad and dirty and betrayed and humiliated. I could never tell anyone what happened to me. Never!

It happened again a few days later. This time I was playing in the attic, dressing up in Granny Ida's old clothes, and Uncle Jess found me. The same scene replayed itself, only this time he removed my clothes. My guilt intensified, my fear multiplied and I became even more rigid in not-thinking. I denied what was happening below my waist, denied that I was being violated and exposed. My shame deepened; I began to withdraw more into my grief and into myself. I cried myself to sleep a lot in those days.

I avoided Uncle Jess as much as possible. He stalked me. He increased his attentions to me under the pretense of ''drawing me out.'' Everyone noticed how quiet I had become and expressed concern. It was hard to get out of going to the movies with Uncle Jess, and I looked like an ungrateful child when I cared nothing for his presents. It was incredibly painful to me to be so apart from my mother, especially since I no longer had my daddy. It was terrible to be so misunderstood and not to be able to tell her why. I missed my mother, missed the sharing we had had. I was in prison inside myself, I felt, and was condemned never to be released.

I don't remember how long this went on, but I failed in school that year and was held back. My mother was concerned about me, as was the whole family. They were all kind and loving.

Then the snow came again, and I got scarlet fever. I was very ill for many weeks. I lost most of my hair and was terribly weak. I had a tutor for a long time because I was too weak to return to school. The good part of the illness was that it relieved me of the necessity of avoiding Uncle Jess. I wasn't molested in the sickroom.

Before I returned to school in the Spring, my uncle was caught disrobing a neighbor's seven-year-old daughter. She too had been afraid to tell her mother, and Uncle Jess had been taking advantage of her fear and shame for a long time.

My mother was devastated. She loved her brother, and stood by him. He was sent away; it was devastating for Jess, too, because a couple of months after arriving at the asylum he managed to hang himself with a rope made of strips torn from his bathrobe.

I haven't thought of this for many years. But Bobby came to visit us this week. I wonder if he thought it strange that I snatched my daughter from his lap as he sat stroking her hair.

# Appendix A
# Resources

**Anatomically Correct Dolls**

Analeka Industries, Inc.
P.O. Box 141
West Linn, OR 97068
    Male and female adult, male and female juvenile.
    Available in black and white.

Migima Designs (503) 726-5442
P.O. Box 70064
Eugene, OR 97401
    Doll patterns, adult and child. Films, training materials and cassettes,
    "Interviewing the Young Sex Crime Victim With the Aid of Dolls," and
    "Talking to a Child About Preventing Sexual Molestation."

Teach-A-Bodies (817) 923-2380
2544 Boyd Street
Fort Worth, TX 76109
    Male and female adult, child and toddler.
    Available in black and white.

Teach-A-Bodies (817) 923-2380
2544 Boyd Street
Fort Worth, TX 76109
    "Teach-A-Bodies: An Effective Resource for Sex Education, Investigation,
    Therapy and Courtroom Testimony." Booklet demonstrating use of dolls.

**Books and Pamphlets**

Bassett, K. "My Very Own Special Body Book," 1981.
    Booklet for parents to read to young children, to teach respect for their bodies
    and the differences between appropriate and inappropriate touch.
        Kerry Bassett
        % Hawthorne Press
        P.O. Box 3910
        Redding, CA 96049

Booraem, C. et al. "Help Your Child Be Self-Confident," 1978.
    Techniques to teach children assertiveness.
        Prentice Hall
        Englewood Cliffs, NJ 07632

Chetin, H. "Frances Ann Speaks Out: My Father Raped Me," 1977.
    Booklet for children on sexual abuse.
        New Seed Press
        P.O. Box 3016
        Stanford, CA 94305

Christy, K. "Sexual Misuses of Children: Tools For Understanding," 1978.
Manual for parents and professionals containing exercises to use with children.

> Pierce County Rape Relief
> Allenmore Medical Center #8-2002
> 19th and Union
> Tacoma, WA 98405

Dayee, F.S. "Private Zone: A Book Teaching Children Sexual Assault Prevention Tools," 1983.
Booklet for children aged 3-9 focusing on good and bad touching and self-protection.

> The Charles Franklin Press
> 18409-90th Avenue W.
> Edmonds, WA 98020

Fay, C.A. & Fay, J.J. "No More Secrets: Protecting Your Child From Sexual Assault," 1981.
Book for parents and professionals. Provides concrete guidance on prevention and management of child sexual abuse.

> Impact Publishers
> P.O. Box 1094
> San Luis Obispo, CA 93406

Fay, J.J. & Flerchinger, B.J. "Top Secret: Why Has Sexual Assault Been TOP SECRET?" 1982.
30-page booklet for teenagers

> King County Rape Relief
> 305 S. 43rd Street
> Renton, WA 98055

Fay, J. "He Told Me Not To Tell," 1979.
30-page booklet for parents and professionals to use with children. Topics include talking with children about abuse, helping children protect themselves, and coping when you learn that your child has been abused. Also "Top Secret: Sexual Assault Information For Teenagers Only."

> King County Rape Relief
> 305 S. 43rd Street
> Renton, WA 98055

Haddad, J.L. & Martin, L.H. "What If I Say No!," 1981.
Prevention booklet for children

> Foundation for America's Sexually
> Exploited Children (F.A.S.E.C.)
> P.O. Box 5370
> Hacienda Heights, CA 91745

Kissel, C. & Tibbits, E. "Daddy's Girl," 1979
Four girls discuss molestation by fathers and stepfathers and their involvement in Daughters and Sons United.

> Parents Center
> 532 Soquel Avenue
> Santa Cruz, CA 95060

Project Two. "Ice Cream Isn't Always Good."
    24-page booklet for elementary school children on the dangers of involvement
    with strangers.
                        Project Two
                        P.O. Box 5091-FL
                        F.D.R. Station
                        New York, NY 10150

Sanford, L.T. "Come Tell Me Right Away," 1982.
    23-page booklet summarizing *The Silent Children: A Parent's Guide to the
    Prevention of Child Sexual Abuse*.
                        Linda Tschirhart Sanford, LICSW
                        123 Sutherland Road
                        Brookline, MA 02173

Stowell, J. & Deitzel, M. "My Very Own Book About Me," 1982.
    39-page booklet for young children. Focuses on different kinds of touch,
    feelings involved in molestation, and management. Guides for therapists
    and teachers also available.
                        Rape Crisis Resource Library
                        Lutheran Social Services
                        N. 1226 Howard
                        Spokane, WA 99201

Sweet, P.E. "Something Happened To Me," 1981.
    Booklet for young children. Focuses on feelings of child victims.
                        Mother Courage Press
                        224 State Street
                        Racine, WI 53403

Tegner, B. & McGrath, A. "Self-Defense for the Young Child," 1976.
    Pictures and text on self-defense and assertiveness for children.
                        Thor Publishing
                        Ventura, CA 93001

Williams, J. "Once I Was A Little Bit Frightened," 1980.
    15-page illustrated booklet on sexual abuse. To be read to children. Aids
    in assessment of molestation.
                        Rape and Abuse Crisis Center
                        P.O. Box 1655
                        Fargo, ND 58107

Williams, J. "Red Flag-Green Flag People," 1980.
    22-page coloring book focusing on good and bad touch.
                        Rape and Abuse Crisis Center
                        P.O. Box 1655
                        Fargo, ND 58107

Wooden, K. "Child Lures: A Guide To Prevent Abduction."
Pamphlet describing child lures and prevention.
Child Lures
Ralston Purina Company,
Breakfast Foods Division
Checkerboard Square
St. Louis, MO 63164

**Films, Tapes, Cassettes and Transcripts**
(*Code*: C= Children  A= Adult)

Abbot Motion Picture Library: *Rape Examination*. 16 mm., 20 min., 1976. Chicago, IL
60600                                                                                    (A)

Aims Instructional Media Inc.: *Boys Beware*. 14 min., color. 626 Justin Avenue, Glendale,
CA 91201                                                                                 (C)

Aims Instructional Media Inc.: *Child Molestation: A Crime Against Children*. 11 min.
626 Justin Avenue, Glendale, CA 91201                                                    (C)

Aims Instructional Media Inc.: *Child Molestation: When To Say No*. 15 min., color. 626
Justin Avenue, Glendale, CA 91201                                                        (C)

Aims Instructional Media Inc.: *Roscoe's Rules*. 10 min. 626 Justin Avenue, Glendale,
CA 91201                                                                                 (C)

Aims Instructional Media Inc.: *Sexual Abuse: America's Secret Shame*. 30 min., color.
626 Justin Avenue, Glendale, CA 91201                                                    (A)

Aims Instructional Media Inc.: *Strangers We Meet*. 10 min. 626 Justin Avenue, Glendale,
CA 91201                                                                                 (C)

Aims Instructional Media Inc.: *The Dangerous Stranger*. 10 min. 626 Justin Avenue,
Glendale, CA 91201                                                                       (C)

Aims Instructional Media Inc.: *The Trouble With Strangers*. 10 min. 626 Justin Avenue,
Glendale, CA 91201                                                                       (C)

American Academy of Pediatrics: *Medical Management of the Sexually Abused Child*.
Videotape, 30 min. 1801 Hinman Avenue, Evanston, IL 60204                                 (A)

American Psychiatric Association Press, Inc.: *Incest: New Clinical Research*. #AT-028-2
(3 cassettes), Moderator: Jean M. Goodwin, M.D., P.O. Box 19343, Washington, DC
20036                                                                                    (A)

American Psychiatric Association Press, Inc.: *Therapeutic Intervention in Father-Daughter
Incest*. #AT-029-2 (3 cassettes), Moderator: Judith L. Herman, M.D., P.O. Box 19343,
Washington, DC 20036                                                                     (A)

American Film Advertising: *Sexual Abuse: Identification, Management and Treatment*, Audio Tape, 1978, Part 1 and 2, and *Development of a Community Response System to Sexual Abuse*. Audio Tape, 1978. Six 11th Street N.E., Atlanta, GA 30309    (A)

Aptos Film Production Inc.: *Beware of Strangers*. 16 mm., 20 min. 729 Seward Street, Los Angeles, CA 90038    (C)

BFA Educational Media: *Meeting Strangers: Red Light/ Green Light*. 16 mm. 21 min. P.O. Box 1795, Santa Monica, CA 90406    (C)

Boys Town Center: *Don't Get Stuck There*. 15 min., color. Research, Youth and Public Division, Boys Town, NE 68010    (C)

DACOM Communications: *Boys Beware*. 16 mm., 14 min., color. 626 Justin Ave., Glendale, CA 91201    (A/C)

DACOM Communications: *Girls Beware*. 16 mm., 12 min., color. 626 Justin Ave., Glendale, CA 91201    (A/C)

Donahue Transcripts: *K. Brady/Incest, #11099, #01121*. Donahue Transcript, Department A., P.O. Box 2111, Cincinnati, OH 45201    (A)

Face to Face Health and Counseling Services, Inc.: *Abused Adolescents Speak Out*. Videotape, 1/2'', 26 min. 730 Mendota, St. Paul, MN    (A)

Family Information Systems, Inc.: *Sometimes It's Okay To Tattle*. Videotape, 10 min., 1616 Soldiers Field Road, Boston, MA 02135    (C)

Film Fair Communications: *Better Safe Than Sorry*. 16 mm., 28 min. 10900 Ventura, P.O. Box 1728, Studio City, CA 91604

Film Fair Communications: *No Exceptions*. 16 mm., 24 min. 10900 Ventura, P.O. Box 1728, Studio City, CA 91604

Films Inc.: *Not A Pretty Picture*. 16 mm., 83 min. 1144 Wilmeth, Wilmette, IL 60091

Information Center, Region V, Child Abuse and Neglect Resource Center. *The "C" Case Interviews Conducted in a Case of Incest in a Middle Class Family*. 52 min. Graduate School of Social Work, University of Wisconsin—Milwaukee, Milwaukee, WI 53201    (A)

International Chiefs of Police: *The Child Molester*. Slide-cassette, 20 min., color. 1319 18th Street, N.W., Washington, DC 20036    (A)

Krause House: *Speak Up, Say No!* Filmstrip, cassette and teaching guide. P.O. Box 880, Oregon City, OR 97045-0059    (C)

Lawren Productions, Inc.: *Interviewing the Young Sex Crime Victim With the Aid of Dolls*, and *Talking To a Child About Preventing Sexual Molestation*. Audio cassettes, P.O. Box 666, Mendocino, CA 95460    (A)

Lawren Productions, Inc.: *A Time for Caring: The School's Response to the Sexually Abused Child*. 16 mm., 28 min., color, P.O. Box 666, Mendocino, CA 95460          (A)

Lawren Productions, Inc.: *The Sexually Abused Child: A Protocol for Criminal Justice*. 16 mm., 26 min., P.O. Box 666, Mendocino, CA 95460          (A)

M.A.S.S. Library: *Suffer the Children*. Videotape, 37 min. University of Connecticut, Box U-127, Storrs, CT 06268          (A)

Media Guild: *Incest: The Hidden Crime*. 16 mm., 16 min., color. c/o Association Film, 7838 San Fernando Road, Sun Valley, CA 91352          (A)

Mitchell Gebhardt Film Co.: *Incest: The Victim Nobody Believes*. 16 mm., 20 min. 1976. 1380 Bush Street, San Francisco, CA 94109          (A)

Motorola Teleprograms, Inc.: *The Last Taboo*. 16 mm., 25 min., 1977. 4825 North Scott Street, Suite 23, Schiller Park, IL 60076          (A)

Motorola Teleprograms, Inc.: *Childhood Sexual Assault*. 16 mm. 48 min., 4825 North Scott Street, Suite 23, Schiller Park, IL 60076          (A)

M.T.I. Teleprograms, Inc.: *Incest, The Hidden Shame*. 16 mm., 19 min. Sound motion picture or video cassette. 3710 Commercial Avenue, Northbrook, IL 60062          (A)

M.T.I. Teleprograms, Inc.: *The Sexually Abused Child: Identification/Interview*. 16 mm., 10 min., color. 3710 Commercial Avenue, Northbrook, IL 60062          (A)

M.T.I. Teleprograms, Inc.: *Who Do You Tell?* 16 mm., 11 min., color. 3710 Commercial Avenue, Northbrook, IL 60062          (C)

M.T.I. Teleprograms, Inc.: *Childhood Sexual Abuse*. 16 mm., 50 min., color. 3710 Commercial Avenue, Northbrook, IL 60062          (A)

National Audiovisual Center: *Sexual Abuse: The Family*. 16 mm., 30 min. General Services Division, Washington, DC 20409          (A)

National Audiovisual Center: *Medical Indicators of Child Abuse and Neglect, Part Five: Sexual Abuse*. Sound filmstrip. General Services Division, Washington, DC 20409          (A)

ODN Productions, Inc.: *No More Secrets*. 16 mm., 13 min. 74 Varick Street, Suite 304, New York, NY 10013          (C)

ODN Productions, Inc.: *No More Secrets*. 12 min., color. 74 Varick Street, Suite 304, New York, NY 10013          (C)

ODN Productions, Inc.: *The Date: The Acquaintance Rape Series*. 7 min., color. 74 Varick Street, Suite 304, New York, NY 10013          (C)

Phoenix Films: *Shatter the Silence*. 16 mm., 29 min., 468 Park Avenue South, New York, NY 10016          (A)

Protective Services Resource Inst.: *Sexual Abuse*. Audio cassette, 24 min. Rutgers Medical School, P.O. Box 101, Piscataway, NJ 08854 (A)

S-L Film Productions: *Shatter the Silence*. 16 mm., or video cassette, 29 min., color. P.O. Box 41108, Los Angeles, CA 90041 (A/C)

Society for Visual Education: *Negative Touch: Ways To Say No*. Color filmstrip/audio cassette. 15:45 min. Child Abuse Series, 1345 Diversey Parkway, Chicago, IL 60614 (C)

Texas State Department of Public Welfare. *Sexual Abuse of Children*. Videotape, 51 min., color. Educational Media Production Section, John M. Reagan Building, Austin, TX 78701 (A)

University of Calgary: *Child Sexual Abuse: The Untold Secret*. Video cassette, 30 min., color. 2500 University Drive, N.W., Calgary, Alberta, Canada T2N-IN4 (A)

Women Make Movies, Inc.: *Fear*. 16 mm., 7 min. 257 W. 19th Street, New York, NY 10011 (A)

**Organizations, Self-Help Groups and Directories**

The following provide facts, information, literature and book lists on child abuse and neglect:

American Humane Association
Children's Division
5351 S. Roslyn Street
Englewood, CO 80110, (303) 779-1400

Child Welfare League of America
67 Irving Place
New York, NY 10003, (212) 274-7410

Children's Aid Society
105 E. 22nd Street
New York, NY 10010

Children's Protection Report Directory Services Co.
1301 20th Street, N.W.
Washington, DC 20036
    Offers "The National Directory of Children and Youth Services."

Children's Public Policy Network
Children's Defense Fund
1520 New Hampshire Ave., N.W.
Washington, DC 20036

Dee Scofield Awareness Program
4418 Bay Court Avenue
Tampa, FL 33611, (813) 839-5025
    Search guidance, educational literature and educational photo exhibit on missing children.

152                                                    *SEXUAL ABUSE*

Feminists in Self-Defense Training
P.O. Box 1883
Olympia, WA 98507
    Interested in networking.

Foundation for America's Sexually Exploited Children (F.A.S.E.C.)
P.O. Box 5370
Hacienda Heights, CA 91745

Hotlines
    Child Abuse Hotline (Toll Free) 800-CHILDLINE 923-0313
    National Runaway Switchboard (Toll Free) 800-621-4000
    Parents Network (National Committee for Citizens in Education) (Toll Free)
        800-NETWORK
    Children's Public Policy Network (Children's Defense Fund) (Toll Free)
        800-424-9602
    Child Abuse and Hotline Information (Referral and Support) (202) 628-3228
    Child Find Missing Children Hotline (Toll Free) 800-431-5005

Identification Programs (Medical identification and fingerprinting)
    Child Print, Inc.
    2705 Woodcliff
    College Station, TX 77840, (409) 696-7893

    National Child Safety Council
    P.O. Box 986
    Jackson, MI 49204

    Proof Positive, Inc.
    P.O. Box 398
    Bay City, MI 48707-0398, (517) 893-3393

Incest Survivor's Anonymous World Services
P.O. Box 5613
Long Beach, CA 90805, (213) 422-1632
    Networking, referrals, literature packets.

Institute for the Study of Sexual Assault
403 Ashbury Street
San Francisco, CA 94117
    Publishers of *Legal Handbook for Crisis Centers*, containing information on
    confidentiality in court proceedings, the retaliatory assailant and liability of directors.

Katherine Brady Foundaton
3 Sheridan Square
New York, NY 10014
    Information on how to increase community awareness.

National Alliance for the Prevention and Treatment of Child Abuse and Maltreatment
41-27 169th Street
Flushing, NY 11258
  Develops guidelines for public awareness programs on abuse and neglect.

National Center for the Prevention and Treatment of Child Abuse and Neglect
1205 Oneida Street
Denver, CO 80220, (303) 321-3963

National Center on Child Abuse and Neglect
Children's Bureau, Office of Human Development Services
Administration for Children, Youth and Families
U.S. Department of Health and Human Services
P.O. Box 1182
Washington, DC 20013, (202) 755-8208

National Center on Women and Family Law
799 Broadway #402
New York, NY 10003
Attention: Laura Arbeitman or Joanne Schulman
  Assists in emergency subpoena cases.

National Committee for Prevention of Child Abuse
111 E. Wacker Drive #510
Chicago, IL 60601

National Institute of Mental Health
National Center for Prevention and Control of Rape
Rm. 6-C-12, Parklawn Building
5600 Fishers Lane
Rockville, MD 20857

National Legal Resource Center for Child Advocacy and Protection
American Bar Associaton/Young Lawyers Division
1800 M. Street N.W., 2nd Floor S.
Washington, DC 20005, (202) 628-6800
  Publications surveying state laws and legal issues related to incest, treatment
  programs, and approaches to prosecution.

National Technical Information Service
5285 Port Royal Road
Springfield, VA 22161
  Offers "Child Abuse and Neglect Programs." Lists programs and agencies
  nationwide that deal with child abuse and neglect.

National Urban League
Child Abuse Resource Center
500 E. 62nd Street
New York, NY 10021, (212) 644-6678

Parents Anonymous National Office
22330 Hawthorne Blvd., #209
Torrance, CA 90505

Parent's United
P.O. Box 952
San Jose, CA 95108, (408) 280-5055
    Referrals, support, workshops. Has listing of sexual abuse projects nationwide.

Society's League Against Molesters (S.L.A.M.)
P.O. Box 1267
Chino, CA 91710, (714) 623-2136 or (714) 947-3204.
    Literature, information on forming local chapters.

Treatment for Sexual Aggressives (T.S.A.)
Box 17
722 W. 168th Street
New York, NY 10032
    T.S.A. newsletter for professionals working with sex offenders.

Victims of Incest Can Emerge (VOICE)
P.O. Box 3724
Grand Junction, CO 81502
Attention: Diane Carson, Coordinator, National Network, (303) 241-2746
    Referral, support, self-help groups, membership, newsletter.

**Regional Child Abuse and Neglect Resource Centers (CANRC)**

The following resource centers offer training, consultation, information, printed and audio-visual materials, and bibliographies:

Region I CA/N Resource Center
Judge Baker Guidance Center
295 Longwood Avenue
Boston, MA 02115
(617) 232-8390
(CT, ME, MA, RI, VT, NH)

Region II CA/N Resource Center
College of Human Ecology
Cornell University
MUR Hall
Ithaca, NY 14853
(607) 256-7794 (NJ, NY, PR, VI)

Region III CA/N Resource Center
School of Social Work
Virginia Commonwealth University
1001 W. Franklin St.
Richmond, VA 23284
(804) 257-6231 or 6628
(DC, DE, MD, PA, VA, WV)

Region IV CA/N Resource Center
Regional Institute for Social Welfare Research
P.O. Box 152
Athens, GA 30601
(404) 542-7614
(AL, FL, GA, KY, MS, NC, SC, TN)

Region V CA/N Resource Center
Graduate School of Social Welfare
University of Wisconsin—Milwaukee
P.O. Box 786
Milwaukee, WI 53201
(414) 963-4184
(IL, IN, MI, MN, OH, WI)

Region VI CA/N Research Center
Graduate School of Social Work
University of Texas at Austin
Austin, TX 78712
(512) 471-4067
(AR, LA, NM, OK, TX)

Region VII CA/N Resource Center
National Resource Center on Family Based Services
University of Iowa—Oakdale Campus: N118 OH
Oakdale, IA 52319
(319) 353-5076
(IA, KS, MO, NE)

Region VIII CA/N Resource Center
Graduate School of Social Work
University of Denver
1205 Oneida Street
Denver, CO 80208
1-800-525-0246 (Toll Free) (303) 321-3963 (Colorado Only)
(CO, MT, ND, SD, UT, WY)

Region IX CA/N Resource Center For Children, Youth, and Families
California State University-Los Angeles
5151 State University Drive
Los Angeles, CA 90032
(213) 224-3284
(AZ, CA, HI, NV, GUAM, Trust Terr.)

Region X CA/N Resource Center
Western Federation For Human Services
157 Yesler Way #208
Seattle, WA 98104
(206) 624-1062
(AK, ID, OR, WA)

**School Curricula and Information for Educators**

American Federation of Police
1100 N.E. 125th Street
North Miami, FL 33161
    Offers "Prevention-Missing Children," a 118-page manual of prevention infor-
mation and resource lists for police, educators and parents. Profiles the child abuser
and rapist.

C.A.R.E. Productions
5497—125 A Street
Surrey, B.C. V3W 323
    Kits for Child Sexual Abuse Prevention, K-3. Contains curriculum guide, message
and discussion cards, puppets, posters, audio tapes and books for students.

Child Assault Prevention
P.O. Box 02084
Columbus, OH 43202
    Offers *Strategies For Free Children*, a handbook covering children's rights,
information about child sexual assault, crisis intervention guidelines, classroom
workshops and a feminist analysis of prevention.

Children's Creative Safety Program
Safety Fitness Exchange (S.A.F.E.)
541 Avenue of the Americas
New York, NY 10011
    Self-defense curriculum for children developed by Flora Colao, a social worker
and education consultant, and Tamer Hosansky, a teacher and martial artist. Also,
a parent-toddler program, *Getting Strong Together*, to teach parents self-defense.
Includes instructions for parents to teach children safety and self-defense.

Committee for Children
Judicial Advocacy
530 Wellington
Seattle, WA 98122
Attention: Ruth Harms
    School curriculum entitled *Talking About Touch*. Also available information of staff
training.

Illusion Theatre and School, Inc.
(Hennepin Co., Minneapolis Curriculum)
528 Hennepin Avenue #309
Minneapolis, MN 55403
> Curriculum for elementary, junior and senior high levels entitled *Child Sexual Abuse Prevention Project: An Educational Program for Children*. Developed by Cordelia A. Kent, Special Project Coordinator, 1979. Also offers touch study cards for classroom and home use to encourage dialog and facilitate learning about appropriate and inappropriate touch.

KCPCA
214 W. 6th, Suite 301
Topeka, KS 66603-3792
> Offers *Bubbylonian Encounter*, a 30-minute play on touching for elementary school children.

Learning Publications, Inc.
P.O. Box 1326
Holmes Beach, FL 33509
> Plummer, C.A., *Preventing Sexual Abuse: Activities and Strategies for Those Working With Children and Adolescents*. Guidelines for forming prevention programs, curricula and lesson plans for grades K-6, 7-12 and special populations, pre/post tests and sample letters to parents, 1984.

Lutheran Social Services
Division of Child Sexual Abuse Prevention and Treatment
223 North Yakima Avenue
Tacoma, WA 98403
> Manual entitled *Child Sexual Abuse: Prevention and Treatment, A Manual for People Who Work With Children*. Includes information on starting a community prevention program, treatment practices, and historical and descriptive overview.

Social Interest Press
670 Northwestern Avenue
Wooster, OH 44691
> Mortimer, V.K. *One In Four: Handling Child Sexual Abuse—What Every Professional Should Know*. Includes assessment, medical and legal interventions, prevention and use of anatomically correct dolls.

Tacoma Public Schools
Counseling and Career Development
P.O. Box 1357
Tacoma, WA 98401
Attention: Marlys Olson
> Curricula entitled *Personal Safety: Prevention of Child Sexual Abuse*. Separate curricula for Head Start, K-2, 3-4, 5-6, Junior High, Senior High. Each curriculum contains daily lessons and student activity handouts.

The Coalition for Child Advocacy
P.O. Box 159
Bellingham, WA 98227
> Developed "The Touching Problem," by Sandra L. Kleven and Joan Krebill, 1981,
> 32 p. Details development and activities of theatre group, S.O.A.P. (Serious
> Overtures About People) Box Players' performances in schools. Includes scripts
> and information to help communities develop prevention programs. Videotape also
> available. Also, *Sexual Abuse Prevention: A Lesson Plan*, by Sandra L. Kleven,
> 1981, Five page sexual abuse prevention plan for teachers, K-6.

WAR-Child Assault Prevention Project of Women Against Rape
P.O. Box 02084
Columbus, OH 43202
> Offers information on how to start a prevention program.

Washington Coalition of Sexual Assault Programs
1063 Capital Way #217
Olympia, WA 98501
> *Public Education Manual* for prevention educators. Covers training speakers,
> developing a presentation and resources.

# Appendix B
# Annotated References

Armstrong, L. *Kiss Daddy Goodnight*. New York: Picket Books, 1979.
Personal account of father-daughter incest.

Bass, E. & Thornton, L. (Eds.) *I Never Told Anyone: Writings By Women Survivors of Child Sexual Abuse*, New York: Harper Row, Publishers, 1983.
First-person accounts (stories and poems) of sexual abuse. Written by women of all ages.

Betz, B. "Young Male Hustlers." *The Press*, Vol. 10, #5, October, 1982.
Data on male prostitutes.

Brady, K. *Father's Days*. New York: Seaview Books, 1979.
Personal account of father-daughter incest.

Burgess, A.W., et al. *Sexual Assault of Children and Adolescents*. Lexington, MA: Lexington Books, D.C. Heath & Company, 1978.
Comprehensive study by experts in the field of rape and child sexual assault. Covers interviewing techniques and management.

Butler, S. *Conspiracy of Silence: The Trauma of Incest*. San Francisco: New Glide Publications, 1978.
Covers the scope of the problem as well as psychodynamic and social forces. Emphasizes the trauma of incestuous abuse.

Conte, J. & Shore, D.A. (Eds.), *Social Work and Child Sexual Abuse*. New York: Hawthorne Press, 1982.
Focuses on the role of the social worker in addressing the problem of child sexual abuse.

Densen-Gerber, J. *The Big Issue*. New York: Odyssey House, July 1, 1977.
Data on chemical abuse and victims of sexual molestation.

Elias, R. "Young Female Prostitutes." *The Press*, Vol. 10, #5, October, 1982.
Data on female prostitutes.

Everstine, D.S. & Everstine, L. *People in Crisis: Strategic Therapeutic Interventions*. New York: Brunner/Mazel Publishers, 1983.
Includes chapters on sexual assault of children and adult women victims of rape.

De Vine, R.A. "The Sexually Abused Child in the Emergency Room." *Sexual Abuse of Children: Selected Readings*. U.S. Dept. of Health and Human Services, National Center on Child Abuse and Neglect, Children's Bureau, November 1980.
Outlines procedures for medical personnel including physical examination.

Fairoth, J.W. *Child Abuse and the School*. Palo Alto, CA: R&E Research Associates, 1982.
Covers definitions, causes and dynamics, educational problems of abused children,
the role of the school/educator in child abuse, and corporal punishment in the school.

Fernandez, H.C. *The Child Advocacy Handbook*. New York: Pilgrim Press, 1980.
Covers definitions, skills of a child advocate, parents and children as advocates,
staff persons as advocates, agendas and resources.

Forward, S. & Buck, C. *Betrayal of Innocence: Incest and Its Devastation*. New York:
Penguin Books, 1978.
Overview, dynamics and coverage of father-daughter, mother-son, and other types
of incestuous involvement. Focuses on incest in the context of overall family
dynamics.

Freespirit, M.J. *Daddy's Girl: An Incest Survivor's Story*. Langlois, OR: Diaspora Press,
1982.
First person account of incest experience.

Geiser, R.L. *Hidden Victims: The Sexual Abuse of Children*. Boston: Beacon Press, 1979.
Includes chapters on child rape, sexual misuse of male children and sexual
exploitation (pornography, obscenity and prostitution).

Giarretto, H. *Integrated Treatment of Child Sexual Abuse: A Treatment and Training
Manual*. Palo Alto, CA: Science and Behavior Books, 1982.
Includes an outline of C.S.A.T.P. (Child Sexual Abuse Treatment), PU/DSU
(Parents United/Daughters and Sons United), and Giarretto's two-week training
course for professionals.

Greer, J.G. and Stuart, I.R. (Eds.), *The Sexual Aggressor: Current Perspectives on
Treatment*. New York: Van Nostrand Reinhold Company, 1983.
Includes chapters on assessment, treatment, evaluation and research with focus on
biomedical issues and behavioral laboratories for treating sexual offenders.

Groth, A.N. *Men Who Rape: The Psychology of the Offender*. New York: Plenum Press,
1979.
Exploration of the characteristics of sexual offenders based on extensive sample.

Haddad, J. and Martin, L. *We Have A Secret*. Newport, CA: Crown Summit Books, 1982.
Deals exclusively with sexual exploitation of children (molestation, pornography,
prostitution). Informative and thorough.

Hursch, C.J. *The Trouble With Rape*. Chicago: Nelson-Hall, 1977.
Contains sections on child rape including ethnic backgrounds of victims, relationships
of victims to offenders and overall statistics on child rape.

Justice, B. & Justice, R. *The Broken Taboo: Sex in the Family*. New York: Human Science
Press, 1979.
Covers high-risk families, consequences of incest and treatment strategies.

Kempe, R.S. and C.H. *Sexual Abuse of Children and Adolescents*. New York: W.M. Freeman and Company, 1984.
Covers definitions, evaluation and treatment of intra- and extra-familial sexual abuse, includes section on resources.

Kepler, V. *One in Four: Handling Child Sexual Abuse—What Every Professional Should Know*. Wooster, OH: Social Interest Press, 1984.
Deals with investigation and assessment of child sexual abuse, medical and legal management, prevention and treatment. Includes information on training and resources.

Knopp, F.H. *Remedial Intervention in Adolescent Sex Offenses. Nine Program Descriptions.* Syracuse, NY: Safer Society Press, 1982.
Detailed descriptions of programs nationwide that treat young male sexual offenders.

Kreitzer, M. "Legal Aspects of Child Abuse: Guidelines for the Nurse." *Nursing Clinics of North America*, Vol. 16, #1, March, 1981.
Thorough elaboration of legal aspects. Covers reporting, legal implications, guidelines for filing reports, record keeping, court interventions and guidelines for testifying.

Langevin, R. *Sexual Strands: Understanding and Treating Sexual Anomolies*. Hillsdale, NY: Lawrence Erlbaum Associates, Publishers, 1983.
Details sexual disorders in men and treatment implications.

Linedecker, T.L. *Children In Chains*. New York: Everest House Publishers, 1981.
Detailed elaboration on all phases of sexual exploitation of children.

Mayer, A. *Incest: A Treatment Manual for Therapy With Victims, Spouses and Offenders*. Holmes Beach, FL: Learning Publications, Inc. 1983.
Includes overview, family dynamics, legal implications, and treatment strategies.

McKee, B. *Run-Aways, Throw-Aways*. Scottsdale, AZ: Good Life Productions,Inc., 1980.
Impassioned elaboration of causes of runaway behavior. Personal interviews. Elaboration on sexual exploitation of children, child pornography market and pedophilic activities.

McKittrick, C.A. "Child Abuse: Recognition and Reporting by Health Professionals." *Nursing Clinics of North America*, Vol. 16, #1, March 1981.
Details the role of the nurse in recognizing physical and sexual child abuse. Lists physical and behavioral indicators.

Morris, M. *If I Should Die Before I Wake*. Los Angeles, CA: J.P. Tarcher, Inc., 1982.
Powerful fictionalized account of incestuous abuse by a practicing social worker.

Mrazek, P.B. & Kempe, C.H. *Sexually Abused Children and Their Families*. Elmsford, NY: Pergamon, 1981.
Current information on child sexual abuse. International, multi-disciplinary approach.

O'Brien, S. *Child Pornography*. Dubuque, IA: Kendall Hunt Publishing Company, 1983.
   Includes definitions, statistics, types of exploitation, enticements, symptoms and
   effects, profiles of victims and perpetrators, and prevention.

Orr, D.P. "Management of Childhood Sexual Abuse." *The Journal of Family Practice*,
Vol. 11, #7, 1980.
   Outlines requirements and role of the physician treating cases of child sexual abuse.
   Describes the physical examination, collection of evidence, and lab tests. Details
   venereal disease, prophylaxis and pregnancy prophylaxis.

Peters, J.J. "Children Who Are Victims of Sexual Assault and the Psychology of
Offenders." *American Journal of Psychotherapy*, July, 1976.
   Elaboration on victims. Data on perpetrators.

Renvoize, J. *Incest: A Family Pattern*. New York: Brunner/Mazel, 1983.
   Information on family relationships, causes, incidence, effects, treatment and legal
   implications.

Rooney, T. *Who's Watching Our Children? The Latchkey Phenomenon*. Sacramento, CA:
Senate Office of Research, November, 1983.
   Considers scope of the problem, characteristics and consequences, and the state's
   role in child care.

Rush, F. *The Best Kept Secret: Sexual Abuse of Children*. Englewood Cliffs, NJ: Prentice-
Hall Inc., 1980.
   Places incest in historical, political and social context.

Schmidt, A.M. "Adolescent Female Rape Victims: Special Considerations." *Journal of
Psychosocial Nursing and Mental Health Services*, 19, #8, 1981.
   Guidelines for nurses caring for victims.

Schultz, L.G. (Ed.), *The Sexual Victimology of Youth*. Springfield, IL: Charles C. Thomas,
Publisher, 1980.
   Series of articles on problems, diagnoses, and treatment of child sexual abuse.

Thomas, J.N. & Rogers, C.M. "Sexual Abuse of Children: Case Findings and Clinical
Assessment." *Nursing Clinics of North America*, Vol. 16, #1, March, 1981.
   Thorough elaboration on the nurse's role in child sexual abuse. Covers identifica-
   tion, assessment and intervention.

Thorman, G. *Incestuous Families*. Springfield, IL: Charles C. Thomas, 1983.
   Personal accounts, case studies, intervention techniques and prevention are
   thoroughly covered.

# Index

Michana Conference: On Family Sexual Abuse
5/88